Machiavelli in Context
Part I

Professor William R. Cook

THE TEACHING COMPANY ®

PUBLISHED BY:

THE TEACHING COMPANY
4840 Westfields Boulevard, Suite 500
Chantilly, Virginia 20151-2299
1-800-TEACH-12
Fax—703-378-3819
www.teach12.com

ISBN 1-59803-172-4

William R. Cook, Ph.D.

Distinguished Teaching Professor of History
State University of New York at Geneseo

William R. Cook was born and raised in Indianapolis, Indiana, and attended public schools there. He is a 1966 graduate of Wabash College in Crawfordsville, Indiana (*cum laude*, Phi Beta Kappa). He received Woodrow Wilson and Herbert Lehman fellowships to study medieval history from Cornell University, where he received his Ph.D. in 1971.

In 1970 Dr. Cook was appointed Assistant Professor of History at the State University of New York at Geneseo, the honors college of SUNY. He has taught there for 35 years and holds the rank of Distinguished Teaching Professor of History. At Geneseo, Dr. Cook has taught courses in medieval and ancient history, the Renaissance and Reformation periods, and the Bible and Christian thought. Recently, he has taught a course on Alexis de Tocqueville, as well as freshman seminars that focus on several aspects of African American history and American politics. In 1992 Dr. Cook was named CASE Professor of the Year for New York State. He received the first-ever CARA Award for Excellence in the Teaching of Medieval Studies from the Medieval Academy of America in 2003. He was recently named the alternate for the Robert Foster Cherry Award for Great Teaching, receiving a prize of $15,000, plus a substantial award to his department.

After publishing several articles on Hussite theology and monastic thought, Dr. Cook has, for the last 30 years, focused much of his research on St. Francis of Assisi. Since 1989 he has published three books about Francis and the ways he was represented in paintings in Italy. Dr. Cook has also contributed to the *Cambridge Companion to Giotto* and is the editor of and a contributor to *The Art of the Franciscan Order in Italy*, published by Brill in Leiden, The Netherlands.

Professor Cook spends part of each year doing research and teaching in Italy. From his base in Siena, he works frequently in Florence as well as Assisi. He has taken students from SUNY Geneseo to Italy on eight occasions and conducts study tours for the public.

In recent years, Dr. Cook has been a lecturer and site visit leader for the Young Presidents' Organization, a group of young CEOs from around the world. He has participated in their programs in Florence, Prague, Istanbul, and Dublin. In 2005 he was invited by the Friends of Florence, a group of philanthropists dedicated to preserving works of art in Tuscany, to make presentations for the group's meeting in Florence.

Dr. Cook has directed 10 Seminars for School Teachers for the National Endowment for the Humanities (NEH) since 1983; six have had St. Francis as their subject and have been conducted in Siena and Assisi, Italy. In 2003 he directed an NEH seminar for college teachers in Italy entitled "St. Francis and the Thirteenth Century." This seminar will be repeated in the summer of 2006.

In addition to his research in Italy, Professor Cook has studied the writings of Alexis de Tocqueville. This interest came about primarily after his unsuccessful run in 1998 for a seat in the U.S. House of Representatives. He has authored two volumes of local history and writes a weekly column for his local newspaper. He was a frequent contributor to the editorial pages of the *Rochester Democrat and Chronicle* in 2004–2005.

Table of Contents
Machiavelli in Context
Part I

Machiavelli in Context

Scope:

Niccolò Machiavelli (1469–1527) is a name that triggers powerful responses, even from people who have never read a word of his writings. The adjective *Machiavellian*, found in English as early as the Shakespearean era, conjures up the image of an amoral (at best) political leader, wheeling and dealing and lying to achieve his ends—and often sinister ends at that. The historical figure Niccolò Machiavelli certainly would not recognize that interpretation or caricature of what he wrote and believed.

Everyone who has seriously studied the works of Machiavelli agrees that he was a dedicated republican, that is, someone who believed in the superiority of a republican form of government, defined as a mixed constitution with elements of monarchy, aristocracy, and democracy. Machiavelli's own career in government service was during a republican revival in his hometown of Florence following the expulsion of the Medici in 1494. Yet most people today know Machiavelli *only* as the author of *The Prince*, a work he wrote immediately after he went into a semivoluntary exile following the return of the Medici to power in Florence in 1512. In that short work, Machiavelli implores the Medici to exercise strong and, if need be, ruthless leadership in Italy and to expel the "barbarians" (foreign troops). This counsel hardly sounds like the exhortation of a devoted republican. However, once we recover the *context* of the writing of *The Prince* and analyze it, along with a longer work started about the same time, his *Discourses on the First Ten Books of Livy*, we will see clearly that *The Prince* can be read as a book designed to guide leaders in the creation—for Machiavelli, the restoration—of republican government in Italy.

Before exploring the corpus of Machiavelli's writings, we will need to examine three distinct types of background. First, we shall consider Florence and its political history before and during Machiavelli's lifetime. Second, we will look at the developing culture in Machiavelli's time, which we usually call the Renaissance, focusing on how writers and political leaders made use of ancient political thought. Third, we will examine Machiavelli's life story. In doing so, we will focus on his education, his service to the Florentine Republic, and his years in exile on his estate a few miles south of Florence and how each of those periods of his life affected the writings he has left for posterity. When possible, we will glance at Machiavelli's personal letters to grasp how he reacted to the world around him.

Only after laying these foundations can we profitably consider Machiavelli's most important writings. Ideally, we would survey each of his surviving books, even including his plays. However, because Machiavelli's principal legacy is in his political thought, we shall focus our attention on three works that will get us to the heart of what this man believed about how human societies should be organized and governed.

First, we will look at *The Prince*. After attempting to reconstruct the reasons that Machiavelli wrote this little book, I shall systematically examine its contents, focusing not so much on its technical advice but on the broad political analysis that Machiavelli provides. Is this a manual for a ruthless prince—we might say dictator—or a work suggesting the necessity for decisive action in an anarchic and chaotic Italy as a prelude to the establishment of a republican form of government?

We shall next undertake a careful analysis of what many scholars consider Machiavelli's most thoughtful and important contribution to political thought, his *Discourses on the First Ten Books of Livy*. This long work is much more than a commentary on Livy's (64 B.C.–A.D. 17) early history of Rome. Often, Machiavelli juxtaposes ancient and modern examples, demonstrating that history cannot be repeated, but its lessons must be adapted to new circumstances. Although a thorough knowledge of the Roman Republic and its most important historian is useful, I shall provide just enough of that background to make Machiavelli's meatiest work concerning republican government intelligible and useful.

Somewhat briefly, we will look at Machiavelli's *Florentine Histories*, written under Medici patronage but hardly uncritical of that illustrious family. We will use this book to bring together some of the elements of Machiavelli's thought that we found in sketchier form in his earlier works.

Finally, we will turn to an examination of the reception and spread of Machiavelli's works. First, we will consider how Machiavelli's works were disseminated and received in his own century. This will lead to a wider consideration of how Machiavelli the republican became known primarily for his *Prince* and how the adjective rooted in his name became a synonym for craftiness and duplicity. We shall also see that Machiavelli's republican thought influenced the development of institutions and values both in Europe and in America. When all is said and done, we must ask whether the work of Niccolò Machiavelli has contributed to the creation and spread of participatory government in the world, or instead, if it has provided a "how-to" manual for those who would concentrate power in their own hands.

Lecture One
Who Is Machiavelli? Why Does He Matter?

Scope:

In addressing the main concerns of the entire course, I will begin by approaching the lecture title questions in two ways. First, I will briefly place Machiavelli in the context of the history of Western political thought. Second, I will address the question of the "real" Machiavelli. Although many see Machiavelli as responsible for justifying tyrannical and underhanded rule, others regard him as one of the greatest and most important theorists to argue for the superiority of a republican government.

I will also address Machiavelli's modernity. He strikes most people as one of the founders of modern thought and has even been referred to as "the first modern man." I will introduce this idea here, but to address it thoroughly, we will need to examine the world of Renaissance Italy, as well as Machiavelli's writings.

Outline

I.   I approach Machiavelli and his writings in two ways, much as Machiavelli approached ancient history.

   A. Machiavelli is a key figure in understanding the Renaissance, especially with regard to political thought.

   B. Machiavelli is an important commentator on how politics works and what republics are.

   C. I am both a scholar of the Middle Ages and Renaissance and someone active in politics, having been a major party candidate for Congress in 1998.

II. For many people today, the adjective *Machiavellian* denotes or, at least, connotes someone who is dishonest and devious, someone for whom the end justifies the means, someone who believes in iron-fisted rule.

   A. This understanding of *Machiavellian* is hardly new, given that the word *Machiavel* enters the English language as a pejorative term in the 16th century.

B. Such a reputation is based almost entirely on a reading or, perhaps, even a misreading of Machiavelli's most widely read book, *The Prince*.

III. However, there are several ways to read *The Prince*, taking into account the purpose for which it was written.

    A. The book was written rather hastily in 1513 for the purpose of showing the Medici family that Machiavelli had a formula for success and that he would be valuable to those who were ruling at the moment.

    B. Given the chaotic state of Italy in 1513, Machiavelli may have thought that having a strong man take charge in Italy was a first step in establishing peace and order.

    C. There are those, especially in the 19th century during the Risorgimento and in the 20th during the time Mussolini ran Italy, who see Machiavelli essentially as an Italian nationalist.

IV. Furthermore, it is wrong to equate Machiavelli's thought with what he wrote in *The Prince*.

    A. Machiavelli wrote several important works.

        1. Many regard the *Discourses on the First Ten Books of Livy* to be his most important work.

        2. His *Florentine Histories*, commissioned by the Giulio de'Medici, is a study of his native land (the Republic of Florence) from its origins to 1492 (when Machiavelli was 23 years old).

        3. These two works, as well as *The Prince*, will be the focus of this course.

    B. Machiavelli also wrote numerous other works, including *The Art of War*, a biography of the Italian military leader Castruccio Castracani, and three plays.

    C. We have hundreds of Machiavelli's letters.

        1. They tell us a good deal about Machiavelli the person.

        2. They often give us additional insights into his political thought.

        3. They show us a richer context for his works.

V. The course will begin by providing a good deal of political and intellectual context for Machiavelli and his works.

A. First, we will look at the history of Florence, concentrating on the events just before and during Machiavelli's life.

B. Next, we will examine the intellectual tradition of Humanism, of which Machiavelli is a part.

C. Finally, I will provide a biographical sketch of Machiavelli.

VI. It is obvious that Machiavelli matters to those who are interested in the history of the Renaissance or the history of political thought, but Machiavelli also matters for those who want to think and act intelligently about politics in our own time.

   A. Machiavelli is often referred to as "the first modern man."

   B. He is widely thought of as glorifying amorality or immorality.

   C. Machiavelli should be thought of as a republican thinker, best expressed in the *Discourses*.

      1. Although we often think of the United States as a democracy, we need also to consider the republican nature of the American Constitution.

      2. We often praise our republican Constitution for its separation of powers and its system of checks and balances.

      3. Many writers about the American experience stress the need for people to act for the common good.

      4. It is often said that different political skills are needed at different times, even if the goals of the state do not change.

      5. In these and many other issues that republicans discuss and debate, Machiavelli has interesting and valuable insights.

VII. This introductory portion of the course will be followed by an analysis of three major works of Machiavelli:

   A. *The Prince*.

   B. *Discourses on the First Ten Books of Livy*.

   C. *Florentine Histories*.

VIII. The course will end with a look at how Machiavelli's writings have been viewed from the time of his death in 1527 until the present.

Recommended Readings:

Maurizio Viroli, *Machiavelli*, chapter 5, pp. 148–174.

Questions to Consider:

1. When you use the term *Machiavellian*, what do you mean by it?

2. When reading a book, how important is it to know the historical context from which the book comes?

3. What might it mean when we call someone "the first modern man," and what is a reasonable definition of *modernity*?

Lecture One—Transcript
Who Is Machiavelli? Why Does He Matter?

When we think of the Renaissance, probably first and foremost, the names of artists come to our head. You walk into Florence and there's Brunelleschi's dome; you go to the Accademia and there's Michelangelo's *David*. You go to the Uffizi, you see Botticelli's *Birth of Venus*, sometimes called "Nude in a Half Shell." So, those are the first images many people have when they think of the Italian Renaissance; however, we also know that the Renaissance is more than an artistic movement or a series of artistic movements. It's really a period of history that's important to us as modern people living in the 21st century for a number of reasons. For those who, of course, focus on literature, they begin the Renaissance, perhaps somewhat unfairly, as medievalists would think, with Dante Alighieri and then go to Petrarch and others, although Petrarch wasn't a Florentine. But pretty soon, you have to come to grips with one of the most interesting, enigmatic figures of the Renaissance or any other period, a fellow named Niccolò Machiavelli, and that's what we're going to be talking about for quite awhile in this series of lectures, this guy Machiavelli. By the way, very often his first name is mispronounced; you've got an accent on the last "o" and that means it's Nicco*lò*, rather than *Nic*colò.

So, Niccolò Machiavelli is going to be the subject of our inquiry. We need to look at Machiavelli not just as a figure of the Renaissance, although he certainly is central to our understanding of what the Renaissance is all about, but also because he continues to be an important theorist, an important commentator, on politics. In other words, we can say that as historians, we cannot ignore Machiavelli. It's been said that his most famous work, for example, *The Prince*, is the most important book of political science ever written. Some would say it's even the first book of political science, although you get Plato scholars and others who would certainly disagree with that by a long time. But Machiavelli's not just important for his historical contributions, what he added to his own time, because Machiavelli continues to be read, but also, streams of Machiavelli's thought have entered into the general, Western, political consciousness. In fact, at the end of this course, I'm going to argue—and from popular images of Machiavelli this will seem odd to some people—but I'm going to argue that there are important elements of Machiavelli in American republican political thought, although it sounds odd to us because of the way we normally think of Machiavelli.

Let me confess to being interested in both of those sides of Machiavelli. First of all, I'm a historian. I'm a medievalist by trade so Machiavelli's sort of a modern guy for me, but nevertheless, it is important, since I teach courses on the Italian Renaissance, simply to deal with Machiavelli in his period right at the end of the 15th century. As he enters into the public world of Florence, he gets his first official Florentine government job in 1498 and he dies in 1527. So the end of the 15th, the early 16th century, we need to look at Machiavelli the writer and Machiavelli, to a lesser extent, the historical player in the activities of the Florentine Republic. But, those of you who have seen, perhaps, other tapes, I've made known that I took a semester off from teaching in 1998 and was a candidate for the U.S. House of Representatives. As you can probably tell by my appearance here, I lost. Nevertheless, I campaigned for six straight months and thought a great deal about modern politics, and commented a great deal about modern politics in public, as a candidate, on television, in ads, and so on. So, I am interested in Machiavelli personally, both as a historical figure whom I teach as part of a very important period of the development of the history of the West, but also as an ongoing, important, political thinker in the Western world and, really today, in the whole world.

Now, how do we conceive of Machiavelli? What's the popular image of Machiavelli today? Despite the fact that the most famous portrait we have of him shows Machiavelli with a kind of enigmatic grin, we don't usually think of Machiavelli as a fun guy. We don't usually think of him as a laugh a minute, a guy you'd sort of like to have a glass of wine with after the end of a long day. We think of him as intense, we think of him as driven, and of course, we think of him as being—well, how do we say it—Machiavellian; somebody who, in some ways, encouraged or at least accepted the notion that dishonesty and deviousness are part of the political life. We often associate with him the phrase, "The end justifies the means," although he never used that exact phrase. We think of him as someone who believes in a prince, in ironfisted, get tough, don't worry about the details of justice, kind of guy. After all, again, from the 16th century on, the word Machiavellian, or Machiavel in its early form, has been part of the English language. Therefore, that is for most people their modern image. If you want to say something to a friend of yours, or perhaps not a friend of yours, if you want to accuse him of being a little bit sleazy, a little bit self-centered, you say, "You know that was Machiavellian of you," or "You're a damn Machiavellian," or whatever it might be.

Let me suggest, however, that obviously, there is a dimension of Machiavelli's thought that we capture with that adjective Machiavellian, as we use it today. However, such a reading of Machiavelli is quite incomplete. First of all, it implies a particular reading of Machiavelli's most famous work, *The Prince*, which he wrote in 1513. I'm going to suggest, both later in this lecture and in a series of lectures on Machiavelli's book *The Prince*, that that is a facile and, at best, partial reading of *The Prince*. It is much more than telling the prince to get tough, knock a few heads, scheme, lie, plot, or steal. That is hardly the theme of Machiavelli's *The Prince*. Obviously, one can pull passages out of the book and quote them and make him sound like, well, a Machiavellian in the way we use that term. But what I'm going to argue is, again, that's a facile reading, a partial reading of *The Prince*. There are a number of ways I would suggest to read *The Prince* that are perhaps more profitable.

First of all, we need to look a little bit at historical context. *The Prince* was written hastily. Shortly after Machiavelli went on a kind of self-imposed exile in Florence following the loss of his job with the return of the Medici to Florence—I'll go into all of this detail a little bit later on—in 1512. Machiavelli sat down quickly at his farm south of Florence to write this book, at least in part, to say to the ruling Medici family, "Hey Medici family, I'm Niccolò Machiavelli. I just lost my job. I understand politics. I understand if you're going to rule in Florence"—and there was a Medici on the Papal throne at this time—"if you guys are going to rule in Italy, you better listen to what I say. I've got a formula that will actually help you to succeed." It is too simple to say *The Prince* is a job application by Machiavelli, but he certainly is saying, "I've got a lot to teach you guys about how to run a republic. I understand this stuff. I've been working at, I've been thinking about it, so pay attention." And, we always need to consider the reason Machiavelli wrote *The Prince* and for whom he wrote it, which were members of the Medici family.

Secondly, Machiavelli looked around Florence and Italy in 1513 and what he sees is a mess. About 20 years earlier, the French had invaded Italy and then it seemed, at least to Machiavelli and many of his contemporaries, that the rest of Italy was also descended upon by Germans, and Swiss, and almost anybody—later on the Spaniards—coming into Italy. Italy's a mess. Italy's really screwed up and, therefore, Machiavelli is very interested in the question, how do we get Italy working again? How do we get it functioning again? How do we restore some sort of order in a world, the Italian peninsula that looks awfully chaotic? Again, it would make no sense to read Machiavelli's *The Prince* without concerning ourselves with the historical context of its writing and the historical context of Italy, and we will indeed do both of those things.

The last chapter of *The Prince* is a call to drive what Machiavelli called the barbarians, all those foreigners, out of Italy. And, he talks about Italy as an idea and therefore, often, especially in the 19th century during the time when Italy became a unified nation and in the first half of the 20th century when extreme Italian nationalism dominated the politics as we know of the Italian peninsula, Machiavelli was looked on as a kind of prophet, a kind of figure who announced a plan to make Italy a nation, to make Italy great again. And so, one of the legacies of us in the 21st century is a lot of 19th- and 20th-century use of Machiavelli as a political thinker about the unity of Italy, about the creation of the Italian nation. In fact, during the so-called Risorgimento in the 19th century, Machiavelli and Dante were the two great figures who were looked at as laying out sort of the theory and the prophecy of a unified Italian state—and again, I'll have more to say about that, especially at the end of the course in the very last lecture. So, looking at that brief list, it reminds us that simply to read *The Prince*—or as people often do, snippets of *The Prince*—without any sense of the context; and the reason for Machiavelli writing is going to lead us to a false understanding of who this guy was and what he had to say.

It's also very important to remember that Machiavelli left us a lot of writings, that sometimes we seem to operate as if *The Prince* is corpus of Machiavelli's writing, and that is far from so. In fact, he would fill a fairly nice niche on a bookshelf with his writings and let me simply suggest something of the scope of those. In addition to *The Prince*, which is a very thin book, we have a book that he began about the same time as *The Prince* that in different translations has somewhat different titles, but perhaps the fullest title would be *Discourses on the First Ten Books of Livy*. Livy was a great Roman historian at the period of the end of The Republic and the beginning of The Empire.

And, even though we only have a fragment of Livy's work, we do have the first ten books of Livy's history, which is from the legendary founding of Rome through the early Republic of Rome. And, Machiavelli wrote a long, long, not quite commentary, but a book based on his reading and his application of Livy to the current event—his reading of early Roman history. It's a very exciting and interesting book. It's a very thick book and, therefore, it's not read nearly as often as *The Prince* is. Furthermore, sometimes it's hard to make complete sense out of reading the discourses because he's discoursing on Livy and if you haven't read Livy and you don't know some of the major players in the history of the early Roman Republic, then his examples sort of wash by us because he assumes that his audience has read or is at least generally familiar with Livy.

And so, this is an under-appreciated book, but if you read what scholars say about Machiavelli, although they will not all agree, most would say—I will say—that the *Discourses* is the most substantial and important book that Machiavelli wrote. There it is very clear—it is out in the open, it's not hidden, it's not something that subtle scholars see—there, Machiavelli makes clear, "I am a republican"—small "r," of course—"I believe in the republican form of government. The Romans had the best form of government, they were the most successful and the most just society, and the fact that we've moved so far away from those Roman republican principals that are so well enunciated in Livy," Machiavelli argued, "that's one way of understanding why we're in such a mess today." And so, we're going to focus quite a bit, even more than on *The Prince,* on Machiavelli's *Discourses*, and I think we'll find that's an exciting thing to do.

Toward the end of his life, Machiavelli wrote a history of Florence, actually commissioned by the Medici. He never got a real job back, in terms of being in power in the Medici period of Florentine rule, but he did sort of make his peace with the Medici and they commissioned him to write a history of Florence, starting from the beginning when Florence was founded in Roman times and the book ends with the death of Lorenzo the Magnificent in 1492, when Machiavelli himself was actually 23 years old. And so, in a discussion, somewhat brief in this course, but nevertheless a real discussion of the Florentine histories, the title is sometimes translated a little bit different—*The History of Florence* or whatever—but I'm using a translation that translates the title *As Florentine Histories,* plural. We are going to be seeing Machiavelli the historian of his own hometown and also, of course, of his own nation, since Florence was an independent nation, or we might say better today city-state. So, those are the works we're going to focus on and I'm going to be doing sort of real commentaries on in this course—*The Prince, The Discourses,* and *The Florentine Histories.*

However, that hardly all together makes up the body of Machiavelli's work. For example, he did not publish *The Discourses* or *The Prince* in his own lifetime. He did publish one political work called *The Art of War.* He wrote a biography of a 14th-century military leader in Italy, Castruccio Castracani. He wrote a lot of letters. He wrote some plays. He wrote a lot of political materials, as he was an employee of the Florentine government between 1498 and 1512. And so, there is a large body of work; I'm going to try to draw indirectly on some of those things. The letters are of particular import and, by the way, they've just been made available in an English translation—the first English translation of the entire correspondence to and from Machiavelli—and they certainly help fill in some of the personal history of Machiavelli, what he's thinking at the time. I am going to be quoting at some length from one of those letters—the most famous one, written at the time that he was writing *The Prince*—to give us an idea of how that body of material is useful in informing us on who this Machiavelli guy is and sort of what's going on in his head beyond what he formally puts on paper, with the expectation of it being published, being made public.

And so, we do need to appreciate the fact that Machiavelli is not just the guy who wrote *The Prince,* but he is the author of a considerable body of literature and the more we read, in a sense, the more complex Machiavelli gets. The more fully we get to know a guy who can do everything from write an intensely political treatise, to be a brilliant historical commentator, to give us a look at his day-to-day life, and even to describe—in somewhat vulgar detail in one of his letters—one of his sexual encounters with a prostitute. We get a fuller picture of Machiavelli the more that we look at all of his writings.

And so, how am I going to go about setting the context for you before we begin to read *The Prince,* and *The Discourses,* and *The Florentine Histories*? First, in the very next lecture we're going to be looking at the history of Florence. You better hold your breath because we're going to do about 1500 years in 30 minutes, so I'm probably going to leave out a detail or two. But nevertheless, we need to look at this city, of which he is a part, this city in which he is such a patriot—this city in which the Machiavelli family is a very old and well-established family. Secondly, if he lives in Florence during the Renaissance, we need to define not only what Florence is, but what the Renaissance is, particularly focusing on the intellectual movement or what's been called the educational program of the Renaissance, which we call Humanism. Therefore, I'm going to try to present Machiavelli as a humanist thinker. In order to do that, we need to take some time out and ask exactly what we mean by the terms "humanist" and "Humanism." Finally, before we begin—before we get all revved up looking at the writings of Machiavelli—I will give one lecture that will be the biography of Machiavelli, looking at his life from the date of his birth, 1469, the year that Lorenzo the Magnificent de Medici takes power in Florence, until his death in 1527. And, we'll get to know him a little bit personally. We'll get to know about his career and we will be able to order and contextualize into his life, as well as into the intellectual and political context of what's going on in Florence, the writings of Niccolò Machiavelli.

It's clear that Machiavelli matters. He matters to those who are interested in the history of the Renaissance. He matters to people who are interested in politics in our own time. And, I want to reiterate some of the ideas behind the statements that not only Machiavelli mattered, but that he matters for us as well. Machiavelli, so famous, has been written about so many times, by so many people, in so many contexts, that we find that one of the many phrases that's gotten attached to him is that he's the first modern man. Now, that's a hell of a mantle to hang on anybody, that he's the first modern man, and obviously any phrase like that is something of an exaggeration. It dramatizes the break he made with his own tradition. It de-emphasizes continuity. It takes away from the real contributions of many other thinkers in Florence, in Italy, in other parts of Europe, in terms of how we try to understand the break between then and now, between the ancient and medieval world, on the one hand, and modernity on the other. But nevertheless, if you're going to hang that tag, the first modern man, on somebody, then Machiavelli is a credible candidate and we're going to explore why that is. In what ways does he break from a long tradition of political thought, of republican political thought, that we can trace back to the ancients—we can trace back to Aristotle, we can trace back to Cicero? And, how is it that Machiavelli really is somebody and something new?

Machiavelli matters because we so often associate him with glorifying—I'm simply saying what I said before in different words—glorifying amorality or immorality, at least among those who rule and that's an important issue. It's not a completely new issue; Plato talked about the idea of whether there was such thing as a noble lie or not. But, some of the counsels of Machiavelli that we'll look at in detail certainly sound like he's saying that for a leader, anything goes. What he certainly is saying is that the idea that there's a traditional, personal morality, and that political morality is simply morality writ large—Machiavelli is saying that doesn't work. It's not a description of reality and is a prescription for disaster that, as a ruler, one needs to operate by a somewhat different code than one operates as a private citizen—as a dad, or a mom, or a husband, or a wife. And, one of the things that we can see is not totally new in Machiavelli is the development of the notion that, somehow, there are different moral realms, public and private, with sort of different playing rules. You can't simply say one is the extension of the other, but rather they have to work differently because some of the things that might make you a good person will make you a bad and unsuccessful ruler and vice versa. So, we're going to have to deal with the question, is Machiavelli introducing a new political morality? Is he really amoral, without morals, or is he immoral by saying sometimes it's okay for princes to lie, to be cruel, and whatever? These are important questions. They mattered in the 16th century; they matter now.

I also want to take up the issue that Machiavelli, as I suggested especially from *The Discourses*, is an important republican thinker. And, we all know however democratic we are as a nation, that our nation was founded as a republic; think of the Pledge of Allegiance, "And to the republic, for which it stands." We know that when we read Madison and the other framers of the Constitution, Madison was terrified of at least an Athenian-style democracy and praised the republic. Those who argued for the ratification of the Constitution even took on Latin names that were the names of Roman thinkers of the Republican Period. And so, we have to ask, doesn't Machiavelli matter as a republican thinker to us since we live in a republic—a democratic republic to be sure—but nevertheless a republic?

How are some of the ways in which Machiavelli's thought may matter to us who live in a republic? Well, one of the things we praise ourselves and our Constitution for is that we have a system of checks and balances, a system in which one part of the power is modified or controlled by another, and that's something Machiavelli is very interested in. Again, more in *The Discourses* than in *The Prince*, but he's very interested in what we would call—it's not his phrase—a system of checks and balances. We very often talk about, in our republic, a need for people to operate for the common good. It's a phrase we hear over and over again. Well, Machiavelli talks a great deal about the common good; about doing things for the good of the whole rather than the good for any one part and, therefore, that's another part of Machiavelli's thought that might contribute to us thinking about ourselves and understanding ourselves. Another thing we constantly hear in our American politics is that different political skills are needed in different eras. That is to say, you needed a certain kind of president because of a certain kind of situation—whether it was World War II, or the Cold War, or the boom of the 90s, or whatever it was—and somebody who might have been great in one era, those skills might not have served him well as ruler of another era when different skills were needed. That's something we often talk about; we might say it today, finding the right person for the right political job at the right time. Machiavelli talks a good deal about the fact that different skills are needed at different times and whether it is possible, and to what extent it's possible, for people to adapt to changing situations. Machiavelli will examine that in some detail.

So, what I would argue is, if we are interested in the history and practice of republicanism—if we're interested in what we usually mean when we use the word republic—Machiavelli, historically, has been a contributor to the development of republican thought in the West and Machiavelli is a commentator that has insights for us today in the 21st century. We will not find those insights if we simply say, "Ah, let's look at a few snippets. Let's look at the highlights reel of Machiavelli's *The Prince*."

So, let me reiterate as I bring this lecture to a close, again, what we're going to do. I'm going to provide a good deal of background. Once again, it's going to be the history of Florence, the history of Renaissance thought, which we're going to call Humanism or Humanist thought, and biographical information on Niccolò Machiavelli. Then, we're going to turn systematically to a reading, a very close reading, what some today…a term I like to call text crawling. We're going to go through the text slowly. We're going to stop and think about certain passages of three major works of

Machiavelli: *The Prince, The Discourses on Livy,* and Machiavelli's *Florentine Histories.* And, only when we have looked at those works in some detail, alas at the end of 24 lectures, you're going to say, "Damn it, just getting started on this Machiavelli guy. I wish we had more time." Of course what I'm going to say at that point is, "Get the books and read them." Hopefully, this lecture course will, among other things, prepare you to be a good reader of those and other works of Machiavelli. Finally, we're going to close this course with a look at Machiavelli's thought, after Machiavelli is laid in his tomb— by the way, which you can go visit in the Church of Santa Croce in Florence. We're going to look at the reception of Machiavelli's thought in his own century, the 16th century; he dies in 1527. We're going to look at in English republican thought. I'm going to talk about Machiavelli's thought as it comes into the American discussion and discourse about representative government and republican government, and then, again, we're going to say what role might Machiavelli play in making us better thinkers and players in the political realm in the years 2006 and for many years after that. That's the goal. I welcome you along. It's going to be a good trip. It's going to be fun.

Lecture Two
Machiavelli's Florence

Scope:

When people stroll around Florence even a bit, they are introduced to such Florentines as Brunelleschi, Donatello, and the Medici. Stepping into the church of Santa Croce, they see the tombs of Michelangelo, Dante (actually he is not in that tomb), Galileo, and Machiavelli. It is impossible not to be overwhelmed by the great Florentine geniuses who shaped Western thought.

What sort of place was Florence in the period we call the Renaissance? It was an oligarchical republic, and for much of the period after 1434, it was dominated by one family—the Medici. Florence was also a prosperous city, famous for its cloth and banking industries. It was an independent "nation" and, therefore, was constantly trying to gain advantage over its Italian neighbors, as well as deal with the great European monarchies.

Outline

I. Like almost all Italian cities, Florence was founded during ancient times by Romans.

　　A. There was a debate during the Renaissance as to whether it was founded in the time of the republic or the empire.

　　B. There were even claims of Florence's Etruscan origins.

　　C. It was not a particularly important Roman town.

　　D. In late antiquity, Florence, like most Roman cities, became the seat of a Christian bishop.

II. In the early Middle Ages, Florence, again like most Roman towns, was reduced in population and subject to attacks, for example, by the Ostrogoth Totila in the 6th century.

III. When population began to increase in Europe in the 11th century, the coastal cities, such as Pisa, Genoa, and Amalfi, began to grow and to develop trade and civic institutions before Florence and other cities in the interior of the peninsula.

IV. In the 12th and 13th centuries, Florence essentially became an independent political entity, often categorized as a city-state.

    A. Civic institutions developed and took over some functions that had traditionally been in the hands of the bishop.

    B. Florence became a city that manufactured cloth, and the Arno River gave merchants access to the Mediterranean.

    C. Florence's population grew rapidly in the 13th and early 14th centuries, necessitating an expansion of the city's walls.

    D. Although the civil government was in the hands of a rather small elite at the beginning, by the middle of the 13th century, the middle class (lesser merchants primarily, known as the *popolo*) began to assert itself and develop its own institutions.

    E. Florence's social and political divisions lined up with factions throughout Italy that supported the pope (Guelfs) and Holy Roman Emperor (Ghibellines).

        1. Florence was a Guelf city.

        2. Twice in the 13th century, the Ghibellines took over the rule of Florence for a few years.

        3. When the Guelfs ultimately won out permanently, they split c. 1300 into White and Black factions, so named because a woman in one of the factions was named Bianca, "white" in Italian.

            a. We have good sources in the form of chronicles that inform us about these factional disputes.

            b. Dante, Florence's greatest poet, was involved in the White/Black struggle and was exiled from Florence in 1301.

V. The 14th century saw important developments in Florence, in terms of internal politics, foreign relations, and culture.

    A. Florence expanded its territory and sought to gain control of Pisa and other cities in Tuscany.

    B. Although Florence was normally allied with the pope, there were exceptions, especially because, for most of the century, the papacy was centered in Avignon.

    C. Florence became the leading banking city of Italy and Europe, but there were significant bank failures in the 1340s.

D. In 1342, Florence brought in a strong man to rule, a Frenchman named Walter of Brienne, duke of Athens, but soon realized the mistake and expelled him.

E. The Black Death caused the death of perhaps half of Florence's population in 1348, eventually killing two-thirds or more of the population by 1427, and attacks of the bubonic plague continued through the 15th and 16th centuries.

F. There was social unrest in the later 14th century, leading to violence in the years 1378–1381, with the temporary victory of wool workers.

G. A more restricted government was established in 1381.

VI. The 15th century in Florence was dominated by the Medici family.

  A. Although briefly exiled in 1433, Cosimo de'Medici returned to Florence and, though a private citizen, took control of the city in 1434.

  B. For 30 years, Cosimo held firm power, largely by controlling the bags from which names of most public officials were chosen.

  C. Although Cosimo was well loved and was lavish in his patronage in Florence, the city was nevertheless a republic more in name than in fact.

  D. Cosimo was succeeded by his ill son Piero for five years (1464–1469) before Piero's son Lorenzo took charge of Florence.

  E. Machiavelli was born in 1469, the year that Lorenzo became the leader of Florence.

  F. Although Lorenzo was well loved, there was opposition to the Medici, and it became violent with the Pazzi conspiracy in 1478, in which Lorenzo barely escaped assassination, and his brother, Giuliano, was murdered in the cathedral.

  G. Shortly after Lorenzo's death in 1492, the French invaded Italy.

  1. Lorenzo's son Piero did not deal well with the French.

  2. Piero was driven out of Florence.

VII. In 1494 Florence reinstituted a republic.

  A. It was backed by a dynamic preacher, Girolamo Savonarola.

B. In 1498 Savonarola was executed in the main square of Florence.

C. A few days later, Machiavelli took an important post in the republic.

D. The leader of the republic at the time was Piero Soderini.

E. In 1512 the Medici regained control of Florence.
  1. Machiavelli lost his job with the end of the republic.
  2. After a brief arrest, Machiavelli went into a voluntary exile on the family estate just south of Florence.
  3. It was there that he wrote *The Prince* and the *Discourses*.
  4. Machiavelli eventually became reconciled to Medici rule but never again held a major post in the government.

F. In 1527 the Medici were again sent packing, and a new republic was established.
  1. Machiavelli hoped to get his old job back but did not.
  2. Within a few months, Machiavelli was dead.

Recommended Readings:

Articles by Nicolai Rubenstein, Elena Fasan Guarini, and Giovanni Silvano, in *Machiavelli and Republicanism*, Gisela Bock, Quentin Skinner, and Maurizio Viroli, et al., eds., pp. 3–70.

Questions to Consider:

1. Given the history of Florence, how can we distinguish between medieval and Renaissance Florence?

2. How might centuries of political instability and change influence Machiavelli and his conception of a just state?

3. How important is the Medici family in Florence during the life of Niccolò Machiavelli?

Lecture Two—Transcript
Machiavelli's Florence

Florentine history, from the beginnings to about 1530—hold on to your hat, we're going to go pretty quickly, hopefully intelligibly, as we take a look at the development of this important city. If you have been to Florence, you might not be able to see that Florence was like almost all cities in Italy today, a Roman city, because none of the Roman ruins, unlike the city of Rome itself, can be seen as you walk along the street. Nevertheless, if you've been to Florence, there is some evidence that Florence is a Roman city because it's laid out like a Roman city. If you go to the area between the cathedral and the Arno River, you'll notice, for example, the streets are all straight—at least for a while—and at right angles to one another. And, you will notice there's a great big rectangular piazza between the cathedral and the Arno River—today called the Piazza Della Republica—that was, in fact, the old Roman forum of the ancient Roman town that today we call Florence. By the way, once you get outside of that old Roman town, as you're walking around Florence today, that's when the streets start going at funny angles, that's when the piazzas are irregular in shape, that's when you get winding streets, and that's when you can no longer go around the block.

Exactly when in Roman times Florence was founded was an issue of great debate, not just historical but ideological debate in the late Middle Ages and the Renaissance. Dante had, in some ways, assumed that Florence was a city that came from the days of the Roman Empire because Dante admired the Roman Empire. But, by the 15th century, the Florentines had discovered or semi-discovered documents that showed that Florence was, in fact, a republican Roman foundation because, of course back then in the 15th century, the Florentines saw themselves as a republic and, therefore, it was their tradition since the beginning. There were even arguments during the Renaissance that Florence had Etruscan origins before the time of Rome, but one thing we can say for sure is that Florence wasn't a very important Roman town. It was just another Roman town. It is important to say, however, that by late antiquity, 4th and 5th centuries, Florence like other cities in Italy had become the seats of bishops. That becomes important because as the Roman Empire in the West collapses and urban life somewhat disintegrates following the collapse of Roman authority, one of the *raison d'etre* for the existence of places like Florence was it was a religious center. It was a place where the church was administered from, for a bishop administered not just the city, but the territory around it called a diocese. So, Florence has both a Roman origin and, also, it is a real and important place since early Christian times.

In the early Middle Ages, like most cities in Italy, Florence was reduced in population and subject to attacks. For example, the Ostrogothic ruler Totila seems to have come in and done a great deal of damage to Florence in the 6th century. And, we know relatively little about Florence, as well as, again, many other Italian cities in the early Middle Ages. But, in the 11th century, the population of Europe—and Italy, in particular—began to increase and, of course, there's more of an urban tradition in Italy than there was in the rest of Europe, especially when you get very far away from the Mediterranean. But, it was the costal cities, not the inland cities like Florence, that were the first to really emerge as new urban realities in the 11th and early 12th century; Pisa, Genoa, Amalfi, and so on, really did take on a new and somewhat international importance before Florence did. But, Florence did begin to develop its civic institutions and it began to grow significantly in the 12th century. It became a cloth-manufacturing city, something that was possible to do because of the fact that the Arno River flows through Florence providing the water that is needed for the making of fine woolen cloth. And, as the city began to expand, in fact in the 12th and 13th and early 14th century, it got two new sets of walls as it got bigger and bigger and bigger—so too did new civic institutions arise.

First, a fairly elite group of wealthy merchants and urban people tried to wrest authority from the bishop and there were contests between, what we would call, the civil government and the ecclesiastical government of Florence. That's important because we need to realize not just in Italy, generally with the pope, but in all of the city-states like Florence, there continued to be, all the way through Machiavelli's time—remember he dies in 1527—there continued to be struggle between ecclesiastical and secular power because the bishop, in his kind of power vacuum in the early Middle Ages, essentially became the governor of a city like Florence. Of course, like all governors or all institutions of government, he did not want to easily yield power to some new set of authorities. In the 13th century, what we have is a broader kind of government beginning to develop in Florence because you get a lot of, what we would today call, middling merchant. Not the great wool merchants, not the great international traders but these are people who make purses or belts or things that were, by and large, for local consumption. This sort of middling group of folks whom we call by the Italian word the *popolo*, the people. This does not mean the very lowest rungs on the social ladder in Florence, but it's sort of middle class.

What we call the *popolo* began to demand some role in government, some role in the affairs of state in the 13th century, and this led to real clashes because you have still the ecclesiastical institutions that are real and powerful. You have the institutions of this earlier urban elite and now you have parallel institutions very often of the *popolo*. And so, the 13th century and the early 14th century were a tumultuous period in Florentine history. Now, let's make that a little bit more complicated because in the 13th century there was a big, sort of, Europe-wide, ultimately, contest for "who's the boss of Europe," to put it as simply as possible. The contestants are the Pope and the Holy Roman Emperor, although the emperor didn't directly govern France or England or Spain or whatever. Nevertheless, the empire was itself an important entity made up, at least in theory, of Germany and parts of Italy. But, it was also an important symbol of secular political authority. And so, in this clash, which had its most intense moments in Italy between the Pope and the Holy Roman Emperor, especially when by the middle of the 13th century the Holy Roman Emperor was also the King of Sicily. Sicily means the island and southern Italy. Therefore, in a sense, with him being, as Emperor, the ruler of Northern Italy and, as King of Sicily, the ruler of Southern Italy, with the Pope in between, it caused a great deal of difficulty. There were battles and wars and even kinds of Crusades that the Pope launched against the Holy Roman Emperor.

The reason this is important to us is because within the cities of Italy, Florence being one of them, the various factions that were developing there over local issues also took sides in this bigger struggle between the Pope and the Holy Roman Emperor. The terms we use for these two major factions, many of you are familiar with. Those who supported the Pope were the Guelfs and those who supported the Holy Roman Emperor were the Ghibellines. Now Florence was, throughout its history, a predominately Guelf city. That is to say, almost all the time the Guelfs had more power and controlled the city, and the Ghibellines were a kind of political minority and often in exile. There were, however, two exceptions to that in the 13th century when, at least for small periods of time, the Ghibellines did dominate. However, after 1266—incidentally, for those of you who are Dante readers that's the year after Dante was born—after 1266, Florence is a Guelf city again and really always after that time. However, what happened to the Guelf party is what often happened when one side, more or less, totally defeats the other; that is to say, it divided into factions. For very odd reasons, we call those the White Guelfs and the Black Guelfs. The name comes from the fact that one of the women of one of the factions was named Bianca, which is simply the Italian word for white, and so one faction took up that name and, therefore, the other become the opposite, the black. So, that's actually where the names White and Black Guelfs come from. There was a great clash between these two factions of Guelfs right after 1300 and the White Guelfs were expelled by the Black Guelfs.

Most famously, what that meant was that Dante Almightier was sent into exile, an exile from which he never returned and, of course, he wrote all about all of these controversies as well as the earlier Guelf-Ghibelline controversy in his *Divine Comedy*, which I know many of you have read; those who haven't, stop the tape, go out, and read the *Divine Comedy* and then come back and we'll do some more Machiavelli. Dante is a guy you ought to get to know. Now, we know a lot about this period because we have good chronicles, as well as Dante's *Divine Comedy*, to tell us about all of these struggles and, of course, Machiavelli was a great reader of Dante. He loved to read Dante and he knew these other works as well, so that these become the sources for his history of Florence. As you will see, he draws examples from throughout Florentine history in the various books that he writes.

Let's now turn to the 14th century; we're creeping up now toward the century in which Machiavelli was born. There were great changes in Florence in terms of its internal politics, its foreign relations, and its culture. We're going to set the culture aside for a little bit; that's going to be the subject of the next lecture, the development of Humanism. We're not going to talk much about painting per se, but I'm sure many of you know that the early 14th century is sometimes called the Age of Giotto, for example. He dies in 1337. He lives through this period of clamorous Florentine history that I've just described, the end of the Guelf-Ghibelline struggle and the fight between the White and the Black Guelf. I want to focus here on politics because, of course, Machiavelli focuses on politics. Florence sought to expand its territory. After all, it was a city-state surrounded, very often, by enemy city-states—Luca, Pisa, Siena, and Arezzo, for example. There are no natural borders between them, really, as there are natural borders between Florence and what's north of it, with the Apennine sort of curling down and across the northern boundary of Florentine territory. In fact, one of the things Florence desired for a long time was to get its own seaport because although the Arno ran from Florence to the sea, it didn't run through Florentine territory all that time; it emptied into the Mediterranean in Pisan territory. In fact, in 1408, Pisa was captured by Florence, although Florence hardly held on to it all the time after that; it was always an important part of Florentine policy to hold on to Pisa. Again, one of the questions Machiavelli will raise in *The Prince* and *The Discourses* is how do you hold on to Pisa? And, has Florence done it very well? That is indeed a good question.

In addition to being a big cloth-manufacturing city, more and more, Florence became a city of worldwide bankers, replacing its neighbor to the south, Siena, as a principle banker of Western Europe, in general. And so, Florence becomes a center, therefore, not just of manufacturing, but also an economic center of Europe because of the fact that great banking families arose there. Now, in the 14th century, the most important families were the Bardi and the Peruzzi families. They're going to collapse near the middle of the 14th century and in the 15th century, of course, the biggest of all the Florentine banks will belong to the Medici family. But, there was enough political and economic and social strife that in the year 1342, Florence did what many other cities around it had done; it called in a strong man and said, "Okay, take over this mess and rule it." They called in a French man, Walter of Brienne, whom we usually know as the duke of Athens. Don't think of him as a Greek, that's simply his title; he's a French man. As soon as the duke of Athens sort of took residence in Florence, the Florentines said, "Oops, we have made a mistake. This is not a good idea." They drove out the duke of Athens within a year and they always prided themselves. This is one of those historical moments where the Florentines said, "You know, ultimately, we would not give up our liberty. We recognize that liberty is the essential to Florentine people." Again, Machiavelli will look back to this period and see how the Florentines responded in times of strife.

Many other cities called in strong men who essentially never left, and this happened in places like Milan and other cities as well.

In the middle of the 14th century came the most important demographic event of the later Middle Ages and the Renaissance— that is to say, the arrival of the Black Death. There are scholars today who doubt whether it is all or even part bubonic plague, as we have come to be told, but nevertheless, this tremendous demographic disaster happened. Here are the numbers because we need to remember that the Black Death didn't just come once; the diseases continued to appear really into the 17th century. We think that the numbers are something like this; there might have been 130,000 people living inside the walls of Florence before the Black Death in, let's say, 1347. By 1427, we're talking about 30,000 people or at least fewer than 40,000 living inside the walls. Think about that; not all at once, but over the course of several outbreaks of disease, Florence lost two-thirds or more of its population. A town to the south, San Gimignano, over that same period of time lost perhaps 80 percent of its population. So, we need to appreciate the fact that as you can imagine, the decades following the arrival of the Black Death brought about a great deal of social and political turmoil. In fact, in 1378, there was a kind of rebellion in Florence by those who were essentially un-empowered politically, those who were wool workers, but who did not belong to a guild because guild membership was a prerequisite for direct political participation. For three years, there was some violence, there were some murders; there was a real attempt by these wool workers to get control of Florence. Ultimately, they failed and, by 1381, things seemed to have been back to normal—as much as that was possible—and a new constitution, we would say, was established. It was even more restrictive in terms of who were the active political players than the constitution that existed before this wool workers' rebellion, which we know by its Italian name, the Chompi Rebellion.

In the period from 1381–1434, therefore, there was a kind of republican normalcy with a fairly restricted group of participants. One of the families that we begin to take note of—in fact, it even had some sympathies with the lower classes during the rebellion of the Chompi—is the Medici family. They've been around a long time, but they had not been the major players; however, in the early 14th century, there emerges the figure of Cosimo de' Medici. And, although Cosimo was briefly exiled in 1433, he came back in 1434 and that's the date we usually give for the beginning of the Medici domination of Florence. When we think of the age of the Medici, that starts with the return from exile of Cosimo de' Medici in 1434. He was the ruler of Florence for the next 30 years, dying in 1464 and, in fact, being known later on—it says so on his tombstone—as the father of his country, the *pater patriae*. Now, one of the questions that scholars have always been interested in, one of the questions that Machiavelli was interested in, is how did Cosimo govern? What principles of governance did he use?

Well, it's interesting; Cosimo held no office. He was, as he would sometimes sort of say, "I'm just one of the boys. I'm a citizen of Florence like the rest of you." Now, of course, he's the head of the Medici bank, which is the biggest of all the Florentine banks by this time, so he's the richest guy around. He uses a lot of that money for the grandeur of the republic—building buildings, commissioning paintings. For example, if you go into museums, you will discover if you look at paintings that were commissioned in Florence to some of the greatest artists, during the life of Cosimo de Medici, you'll find that two of the most common saints you will find in these paintings are saints Cosmos and Damien, two medical saints. Now, of course, that's nice because this is still the age of this great disease where you might want doctor saints, as Cosmos and Damien were, but let's remember Cosimo de Medici is, of course, named for Saint Cosmos and, therefore, it was a way of glorifying himself. Don't be surprised in the next generation of Medici to find a lot of Saint Lawrences because, of course, it was Lorenzo de Medici, which is simply the Italian for Lawrence, who after all was the Medici ruler for many years toward the end of the 15th century. But, the main way that Cosimo held power was he controlled what names went into the bags from which public officials were drawn. In other words, a lot of offices were decided by lottery and, therefore, the way to control power was to make sure that only people who were favorable to you had their names in the bags. But, being able to control, what were called, the scrutinies, the development of which names are in the bag, Cosimo held great power. It's probably fair to say that although Florence was a republic in name during the time of Cosimo de Medici and following his death for that matter, it was more and more ruled by the strongest man and, of course, the strongest man was a member of the Medici family.

When Cosimo died in 1464, he was succeeded by his son, Piero. Piero sort of gets a bad reputation among historians. His five-year "rule" wasn't very effective and there was clearly some disaffection with the Medici that sort of was a little bit louder and more dramatic during the rule of Piero. Still, Piero was ill the entire time and it may be less his ability than his health that is responsible for the fact that his five-year "rule" in Florence wasn't effective—again, rule is in quotation marks because he didn't hold any formal office. But, in 1469 when Piero died, he was succeeded by his young son, Lorenzo, who many people today still refer to as Lorenzo the Magnificent, and he "ruled" in Florence until his death in 1492. The very year that Lorenzo de Medici became the leader of Florence, a little baby across the Arno from the Medici palace named Niccolò Machiavelli was born. So, he is raised during the period where, again, in form, Florence is a republic. In fact, it is in the hands, primarily, of its first citizen, Lorenzo the Magnificent. Now, despite the fact that we associate Lorenzo with great gentle rule, beautiful art, his own poetry, the founding of educational institutions, and all the rest of it, it is important to remember there was a good deal of disagreement and there was, in fact—and we're going to see that Machiavelli is very interested in this—an important conspiracy against the Medici in 1478 that was aimed at executing, murdering, assassinating Lorenzo and his brother Giuliano. Giuliano, in fact, did die in the so-called Pazzi Conspiracy, but Lorenzo was able to escape. This will be Machiavelli's big story when discussing conspiracies and how they work.

We need to remember that Machiavelli was nine years old when the Pazzi Conspiracy occurred and, once Lorenzo was safe, there was extraordinary public recrimination against those who carried out Pazzi Conspiracy, including people dragged through streets, including people who were hanged out of windows, including the window of the city hall the Palazzo Vecchio in Florence. And, we have to wonder, first of all whether Niccolò Machiavelli actually saw this, but even if he didn't, certainly that was a story that he would have heard not just that week or that month at the dinner table, but the Pazzi Conspiracy would have been one of those stories that would have been told over and over and over again and drilled into him. And, Machiavelli's curiosity led him to think and write a good deal about the Pazzi Conspiracy later on.

Lorenzo died in 1492, was succeeded by a not very talented son named Piero. In 1494, the French invaded Italy. This is one of those draw-the-line dates because after 1494, although this is something of an over-simplification, Italy becomes a battlefield for almost all of Europe. You name a country on the continent and I'll bet you they had soldiers or their king invaded Italy in the next couple of decades—the Spanish, the Holy Roman Emperor, who is German, the French, there were a lot of Swiss soldiers who were there as mercenaries, hence the Papacy had them, hence the Swiss guards that you see in the Vatican today. And so, the invasion of the French is one of those lines drawn in Italian history, in Renaissance history. Piero de' Medici didn't handle the situation very well and was forced into exile from Florence. In 1494, the 60-year rule of the Medici comes to an end and Florence once again establishes a republic, a real republic, with a constitution that was haggled over, partly modeled on the Venetian model, since it was a republic. Florence goes into another period of proud republican history—republic, in fact, and not just in name. One of the great supporters of that republic was a dynamic Dominican preacher—not a native Florentine—in fact from a monastery that had been built in Florence by the Medici, and his name was Girolamo Savonarola. No doubt, the 25-year-old Machiavelli—that's how old he was when Piero de' Medici went into exile—heard those sermons and respected Savonarola, although certainly had none of Savonarola's religious convictions. In fact, in *The Prince*, he hangs the great tag on Savonarola; he calls him an unarmed prophet. In 1498, Savonarola was burned in the center of Florence and a few days later—coincidentally, I might add—Machiavelli got his official job in the Florentine republic. He was named a secretary of one of the agencies of the government.

Now, he therefore entered into the active life of the governance of the republic under a guy named Piero Soderini because he was a de facto and, in fact, later on elected the leader for life of this Florentine republic. Machiavelli worked with him. Machiavelli knew him. Machiavelli respected him, but Machiavelli thinks he really messed up in 1512 by being too shy and not being bold enough when changes were afoot. This is because in 1512, the republic collapsed and the Medici returned to power. That meant that Machiavelli was out of a job and pretty soon he found it, if not necessary, at least advisable, to move to the family estate about 12 kilometers south of Florence in a little village up in the hills towards San Casciano. There, he wrote *The Prince* and *The Discourses*. Although he came into Florence often and ultimately did get some work as a historian from the Medici in the early 1520s, essentially Machiavelli's political career came to an end with the end of the republic in 1512. Here's a guy that believes he knows a lot of stuff, who's eager to serve, who thinks he's got the right prescriptions for Florence, and he doesn't have a job in the government once the Medici take over in 1512. He never has an important post for the rest of his life. In 1527, the Medici are expelled, again, and a republic is established and Machiavelli thinks, "Boy I'm going to get myself a job, maybe even my old job back in this new republic." But, he was passed over, ironically perhaps because he was seen as being a little bit too comfy with the Medici, since he had worked for them in the last years of Medici rule. And, a very disenchanted Machiavelli died in June of 1527.

By the way, to tell you the rest of the story—in 1530, the Medici return and they never leave, eventually becoming the Grand Dukes of Tuscany and remaining the rulers of the Florentine state until they died out in the 18th century. So there we have it, 1,500 years of Florentine history and we'll use that as the political and narrative backdrop for the life and writings of Niccolò Machiavelli.

Lecture Three
Classical Thought in Renaissance Florence

Scope:

The word *Humanism* often accompanies the term *Renaissance*, and to understand Machiavelli, we will have to know what this cultural revival and educational program consisted of. From the very word *Renaissance*, we conclude that there was a rebirth of the ancient classics. Although much of the treasury of Greek literature was rediscovered during the Renaissance, the Latin classics had been read and used throughout the Middle Ages. It is these Latin works, especially the writings of the historian Livy, that Machiavelli was primarily attracted to.

I will argue that the Renaissance can best be understood as an educational movement that approached and found value in the classics in new ways. Thus, Machiavelli cannot be fully understood without a knowledge of the principal tenets of Renaissance Humanist thought and practice.

Outline

I. The word *Renaissance*, which is associated with Florentine culture in the 15th and 16th centuries, means "rebirth," specifically the rebirth of classical antiquity.

   A. The Latin classics were generally known in the Middle Ages.
      1. Often, snippets appeared in anthologies, but many complete works were known.
      2. Generally, the works of classical, pagan Latin writers were regarded as useful—though not sufficient—for seeking God.
      3. Dante, writing c. 1300, clearly was a deep and sophisticated reader of Virgil.

   B. Many of the Greek classics were lost to the West during the Middle Ages.
      1. A few works or parts of works were known in Latin translation throughout the Middle Ages.
      2. The knowledge of Greek was never entirely lost in the West, but those who knew the language were few.

3. In the 12th century, virtually all the writings of Aristotle and works of Greek science were translated into Latin, often through Arabic.

II. The term most associated with *Renaissance* is *Humanism*.

A. This word was not used during the period but is a later invention.

B. It is correct, however, to speak of a new interest in and use of the humanities.

C. Traditionally, Petrarch (d. 1374) has been regarded as the first real Humanist.

D. Recently, scholars have pushed back the foundations of Humanism into the 13th century.

1. There was a renewed interest in and use for Latin eloquence, found in such classical writers as Cicero.
2. The first Humanists, or "proto-Humanists," were not primarily Florentines.
3. In fact, Petrarch has recently been described as a third-generation Humanist.

E. The great writer Hans Baron believed that he could trace the triumph of Humanism in Florence to the beginning of the 15th century, though some scholars have challenged both his basic argument and his specificity.

F. Just about every major scholar would agree that the great age of Humanist thought in Florence is the 15th and early 16th centuries.

III. Humanism involves both the rediscovery of texts that had been lost in the West, primarily works of the ancient Greeks, and new reading and use of texts that medieval thinkers had studied and written about.

A. As mentioned earlier, classical texts in the Middle Ages were largely (although not entirely) used for what was ultimately a theological end.

1. We find in Augustine's *Confessions* (397) a claim that reading Cicero and some Platonist writings were important events in his eventually finding the Christian God.
2. In the 13th century, Thomas Aquinas used Aristotelian logic and content for much of his moral thought and much of his categorization of ethical thought.

B. Even conceding that Petrarch was not the first Humanist, we can nevertheless find in his writings new uses for the classics.

    1. He wrote a letter to Cicero (d. 43 B.C.).

    2. He was inspired to climb a mountain, Mont Venteux in France, to see if he could imitate an experience that Livy described in his history of Rome.

C. At the beginning of the 15th century, the renewed interest in and new approach to the texts of the ancients became central to the writers and political leaders of Florence.

    1. Rome was a republic, and Florence was a republic; hence, the wisdom of the former was seen to be applicable to the latter.

    2. In part, classical rhetoric was important in Florence both within the city and in its relationships with other political entities.

    3. The content was also regarded as valuable in both politics and more generally "the good life."

D. It is important to understand that such uses entailed a new way of reading the texts of the past.

    1. Instead of being seen primarily as works that could guide people to heaven, they were now being viewed as texts that were valuable for teaching people how to live good and happy lives on Earth.

    2. Hence, there developed the idea of a more autonomous realm of ethics in the world.

E. This renewed interest in the classics also involved a search for more texts.

    1. Searches of monastic libraries turned up some new Latin works that had been largely unread and unknown in the Middle Ages.

    2. A great interest was to find and make use of the works of the ancient Greeks.

        a. This move led to a renewed interest in the Greek language, and after the fall of Constantinople to the Turks in 1453, more Greek scholars and books came to Italy.

        b. Many Greek works, for example, Thucydides's *Peloponnesian War* and Plato's dialogues, were translated into Latin.

      c. By the end of the 15th century, the use of the printing press made such works more readily available to those without great wealth.

F. Although there is no rigid division, there is a change in emphasis in the use of the classics about the middle of the 15th century.

    1. In the earlier period, we speak of Civic Humanism, of the application of these new texts to political and social life.

    2. In the second half of the century, there was a more philosophical and contemplative approach to the classics, symbolized by the creation of a Platonic Academy in Florence.

    3. Although Machiavelli was born in 1469, he is more of a Civic Humanist and relied on Latin classics first and foremost and on Latin translations of some Greek classics because he did not read Greek.

Recommended Readings:

Lauro Martines, *Power and Imagination*, chapter 11, pp. 191–217.

Questions to Consider:

1. To what extent is the Renaissance about the literal sense of that term—the rediscovery of lost classics?

2. How might the Florentines see themselves as similar to ancient Greek and Roman societies, hence finding the writings of those civilizations applicable in their present?

3. To what extent is it possible to apply ancient books to a present that ultimately is quite different from ancient societies, and how does one make the necessary adjustment to make such texts useful?

Lecture Three—Transcript
Classical Thought in Renaissance Florence

The Renaissance—it's a term that we use all the time. It's a term that's now used far beyond a particular period of history, but we really need to explore it. Obviously, there are books and there are courses and whatever on this extraordinary period of European history, first in Italy and then in other places. After all, Shakespeare is a Renaissance writer in England. But, we need to look at it in its origins, in its Italian, and in particular, in its Florentine context. In doing that, we're also going to use the word "humanist" and "Humanism" a lot. So, once we understand what's going on culturally in Florence really, beginning in the 14th century and sort of highlighting in the 15th and 16th century—beyond the world of painting, which I'm barely going to mention—then we are going to know the intellectual context in which Machiavelli was born, in which he was raised and educated, and in which he wrote, and to which he was such a contributor.

The word "renaissance," ironically, of course, is not an Italian word, but it's a French word and we all know—we learned this somewhere along the way in school—it is re-nais-sance. It is rebirth, implying that something got born, something died, and something got born again. So, we've got to figure out first, what is it that got born, died, and got reborn and, secondly, is this is an accurate description of what happened culturally and intellectually in Italy, particularly Florence, in the 15th and 16th centuries? One of the mistakes we often make is assuming that if it's the born, died, reborn thing, that means that during the Middle Ages the great classics of Greek and Roman antiquity must have died out. They must have been put aside. They must have been unused. But, of course, that's not so at all. Anybody can tell you that all during the Middle Ages, for example—after all, Latin was the language of learning, Latin was the language of the church—and, therefore, anything that had ever been written in Latin could have been read by the educated people of the Middle Ages. Even a vernacular poet like Dante, living in the early 14th century, not only could read Latin, he wrote books in Latin, as well as writing *The Divine Comedy* in Italian.

So, with regard to the Latin classics, in some very real sense, they didn't need to get reborn because they never died. It is important to say, though, that they were used in the Middle Ages. By and large—

I'm obviously very much generalizing in a particular way—that way being that those Latin classics are valuable because we can use them to learn how to write and how to read text in Latin well, Also, if we use them correctly—especially certain parts of the Latin classics—if we use them rightly, they can lead us toward God, even though they were written by pagans. To put it simply, the classics were an aid although they were not sufficient in moving people toward God. Again, that the classics were taken seriously and that they were taken seriously in the context of Christians seeking salvation is best shown by, again, turning to Dante. After all, through almost two-thirds of Dante's journey through hell, purgatory, and heaven, for almost two-thirds of that, Dante's guide is a pagan, Latin poet Virgil. We can see not only that Dante was a serious reader of Virgil, but a serious reader of Ovid and many of the other great Latin classics.

In contrast to that, let's talk about the works of Greek antiquity in the Middle Ages. Now, we're not going to talk about the Byzantine Empire centered in Constantinople because, of course, that was a Greek-speaking empire and they continued to read the Greek classics as the Latin classics were read in the West. But, the knowledge of Greek, although it never disappeared in the West in the Middle Ages, almost did so. And therefore, for most of the Middle Ages, the only Greek works that were known directly in the West were those that had been translated, or parts that had been translated, into Latin in ancient times. There were, throughout the Middle Ages, little snippets of Aristotle and other Greek writers that existed in the West. But, by and large, the body of Greek literature that we first think of today, we think of Homer, we think of the plays of Sophocles, we think of the great historian Thucydides, we think of Plato. By and large, not entirely, by and large, that body of material was not directly known in Western Europe during the Middle Ages. Now, Dante knew all about Homer in some ways. He knew the plots of the *Iliad* and the *Odyssey*. He even knew that Homer was the greatest poet who had ever lived. But, he had never read Homer. He'd read summaries of Homer in Latin. He read references to Homer in various classical works. He'd even read a few lines of Homer that had been translated into Latin and incorporated into various Latin works, but Homer, he had never read Homer at all.

Now, in the 12th century, the writings of Aristotle, by and large in the form we have them today, were translated into Latin—by the way, not directly from the Greek, but through Arabic. What's important to know is there was this revival of Aristotle. Thomas Aquinas, his writings, theological and philosophical, are unimaginable without both the knowledge of Aristotelian logic and the content of Aristotle's thought. Dante was so familiar with Aristotle that he simply could call him, "The philosopher." He didn't even need to give him a name. So, Aristotle and, generally speaking, works of Greek science were translated into Latin in the 12th century and so that's what exists. I want to point out one specific thing about Aristotle and that is we need to remember that Aristotle wrote about logic; he wrote a lot of things that we would call science today, but he also wrote books on ethics and he wrote a book on politics. Therefore, Aristotle's political and ethical thought became a central part of the Western tradition, again, beginning in the 13th century. So, in many ways, what we need to remember is that by the beginnings of the Renaissance, sometime in the 14th century, in Italy and in Florence, in particular, the Latin classics had always been around, but relatively few of the Greek classics were available at that time and we're going to see how things change.

Now, let me turn to another one of those terms we need to define and that term is humanist or Humanism. Let me start with this: Humanism is not a word that was used in the Renaissance. This is always a problem. Historians are constantly struggling to deal with the fact that words that have come into modern, English usage to describe phenomena in the periods they study are words that have been created in modern times. Gothic architecture, feudalism—those are modern terms; so is Humanism. I'm going to use it because it is convenient, but we need to know that that word is made up by scholars writing about the Renaissance, not by the participants, if you will. But, they did talk about Humanists and the study of the humanities, and that really is what we want to talk about. If you take a look at a broad, general survey of the history of the West, one of the things you will probably read is sometime in the 14th century, we get the beginnings of this new interest in the humanities, in the classics. The figure that we usually use to personify the beginnings of that is Petrarch, an Italian who lived a good deal of his adulthood in France because the papacy was located in Avignon at that time. He died in 1374 and he's sometimes described as the first humanist.

Scholars today have been working on this question of the origins of humanist thought—see, one can avoid saying Humanism if one really tries—and what they found is that, in fact, there are at least people we want to call proto-humanist that go back generations before Petrarch. In fact, there is one scholar who has called Petrarch a third-generation humanist. These earlier humanists, sometimes called proto-humanists, are not necessarily and not often Florentines. Padua is an important university city and a place where we now look for some of the origins of this new interest in and concern for, and use of the writings of ancient Greece and Rome. One of the most popular and interesting theories about the triumph of humanists as the dominant educational program of the ruling class in Florence is by a scholar named Hans Baron. Hans Baron said, "I can trace almost to the year when humanist thought, this new look at the classics, became dominant in Florence. It occurred right following Florence's victory over Milan in 1402, with the death of the ruler of Milan, Gian Galeazzo Visconti. It's very interesting because Milan was about to beat the hell out of Florence. Florence was not doing well and in this sort of great crisis that Florence faced, Gian Galeazzo died and Milan had to withdraw. Then, about a decade later, the Florentines were in a similar kind of situation with the King of Sicily who was located in Naples at that time.

So, the Florentines began to see the triumph of republican Florence over the monarchy or a kind of dictatorship in southern Italy and in Milan. Hooray for the republic, and hooray for republican values, and hooray for the intrinsic superiority of our republican type of society and form of government. How do you learn best how to praise republic? You go back and read the praises and the writings about republic that existed in the ancient world—in particular, of course, the ancient Roman republic. Therefore, in a sense, the classics, the argument is, had a kind of immediacy, a kind of rhetorical immediacy, a kind of theoretical immediacy in Florence because of Florence's self-proclaimed republican triumph over the bad guys; however, much of their triumph was at least a matter of luck as virtue or military power. Now, in recent years, there are scholars who have said, "It's not quite that one-to-one, the triumph of humanist thought and the victory of Florence over Gian Galeazzo Visconti." And so, this is something scholars argue about and the arguments are interesting.

But, at least, suffice is to say that in the early 15th century, what begins perhaps as an intellectual movement of very limited scope becomes a much broader intellectual movement, a new interest in, and use for, the writings of ancient Greece and ancient Rome. If one says, "Boy, is this stuff relevant, boy, is this stuff useful to us here in Florence," what are you going to do? You're going to reread books that have been read for a long, long time from a new perspective and you're going to go hunt for books that might exist that you don't know exist, but that probably exist. And so, that's exactly what happens. We begin a kind of hunt for new writings of favorites like Cicero and a few things turned up. You had people going into monasteries and sort of blowing the dust off the shelf and saying, "Gosh, here's a manuscript that hasn't been looked at for a long time; let's see what's in it. By golly, there's a new letter of Cicero we didn't know about before." So, there were some discoveries of the Latin classics, but there was also a real interest in finding Greek classics because they weren't very well known directly, even though they knew about their existence; they knew about them. So, if you're interested in writing about, and talking about, and orating about, and writing letters about, and living as free people in a city-state, you know those damn Greeks had something to say about that stuff too, especially the Athenians. And so, there became a new interest in learning Greek, finding Greek text, and getting those Greek texts translated into Latin, although learning Greek was the ideal. So, what we begin to have is, literally, a rediscovery of some Greek stuff, and a little bit of Latin stuff, but much more we begin to get a whole new way of thinking.

Let me go back now and review a little bit more the way that people at the end of antiquity—Christians and the early Middle Ages— thought about the classics, so we can see not just that that's going to continue, but that something new with regard to the use of classics is going to be added. If we go all the way back to Saint Augustine who wrote his *Confessions* in the year 397, it is very clear, he makes it unambiguous, reading Cicero and reading Platonic philosophy were important events in his ultimate conversion to Christianity. But, Augustine also warned his readers in many of his works that you've got to be real careful to understand what the classics can't do for you, useful but not sufficient. As Augustine says in Book Seven of *The Confessions*, "I really needed the Platonist to get me over some problems in my thinking, but no Pagan philosopher can take me to God because Christ is the only way to God for fallen humanity." Again, therefore, the classics are useful and certain pieces more than other pieces, I might add, are useful in the journey toward God, but not all and not for their own sake. They're not there for entertainment, they're not there as works to be looked at simply in and of themselves; they are things written by wise men that can lead us toward the ultimate wisdom, which is the wisdom of the Christian god. In the 13th century, in the 1200s, Thomas Aquinas again uses Aristotle—he uses Aristotelian logic and he uses the content of Aristotle—for much of his moral thought and much of his categorization of ethical thought, as well as a lot of Aristotle's science. Dante's cosmology in *The Divine Comedy* is essentially Aristotle's cosmology. So, again, to emphasize, a lot of the classics were very valuable to thinkers throughout the Middle Ages.

Okay, so what's new? What's new in the 15th century? How are people reading Cicero anew? Why do they find it so interesting to go find works of Plato and Thucydides? Well, even though I said earlier that probably we shouldn't count Petrarch as the first Humanist, I nevertheless want to look to him living in the middle of the 14th century as sort of emblematic of what we're talking about here. Petrarch wrote a letter to Cicero. It's a very interesting thing to do because, among other things, Cicero had been dead for 1400 years. Obviously, he didn't sit by the mailbox waiting for a response. But, he wrote a letter to Cicero because he so was taken by what Cicero says and the beauty of Cicero's Latin prose, he felt a certain kind of commonness with him that bridged that 1,400-year gap between them. He had a kind of intimacy with Cicero. Another thing that Petrarch did—he wrote about this in a famous letter—he climbed a mountain in France, Mont Venteux, not too far from Avignon. "Why," he said, "because I was reading Livy," the great historian of the Roman republic. "I was reading Livy one day and in one of Livy's texts, Livy talks about a general who climbed to the top of a mountain and surveys all around him." Petrarch said, "I wanted to have that same experience that that general had. And so I decided I'd climb a mountain in imitation. I'm doing it because it's there and because I'm inspired to learn something and experience something right now. I'm inspired to do that from one of these great classical texts. That passage in Livy just really floated my boat. It turned me on. It got me excited and so I set out to climb this mountain in France to have a parallel experience to what's described in Livy."

That begins to give us a hint of something new about the way the classics speak to us. Not as, "If I read this piece, this might intellectually prepare me for a better reading of the Bible"—although they didn't reject that in the Renaissance—but rather, "I'm going to do this because I'm inspired to imitate and I'm so bound up with the experience that's recorded in some of these classical text"—again, the letter to Cicero that Petrarch wrote—"that I really find a kind of kinship. I feel like there's a way in which we can communicate." I think Petrarch is sort of saying in writing this letter, there's an identity that really goes around that 1,400-year time gap and links us together. Now, to say the obvious, and I said it before, Rome before the time of Julius Caesar was a republic, Florence was a republic and, therefore, especially in kind of the Florentine republican—and I use this word without any bad connotations—propaganda that began to develop, especially after the defeat of Milan in 1402, and these classical authors were directly relevant. They helped to structure our experience in Florence. They helped us to express our experience. They helped us in our diplomatic correspondence, through the Latinity of Cicero and others, as well as the content, and so there was, not just in an individual like Petrarch, but really at the beginning of the 15th century with the elite of the Florentine republic, there was a real sense that these guys, these ancient writers and us are really sharing experiences. We're on a common page. Of course, there are differences. Of course, we're not the ancient Roman republic, but we're founded—Florence was—in ancient Roman times. It is our rightful heritage. And, there is a real sense of the new experience of republicanism that could be understood, furthered, and expressed by using these classics.

Also, what we need to appreciate is, you know, if you read Cicero you say, "Okay, Cicero might help me get to heaven. Helped Augustine get to heaven, pretty good. But you know what Cicero also does? Cicero really helps me live better in this world. I'm a better citizen. I'm a better speechmaker. I'm a better letter writer." Cicero wrote lots and lots of letters. "I may be even a better friend," because Cicero wrote a book on friendship. In other words, without ever dismissing the more medieval notions that reading some Cicero might help me get to heaven, what you have happening at the beginning of the Renaissance is people saying, "Yeah, but Cicero is also valuable in and for himself because he makes my life right here on earth, right now, more successful, better, more pleasant." Therefore, it's really that new sense of the classics as valuable not just in helping me to attain life in heaven, but helping me to live this life well and prosperously and happily and knowledgably, and all the rest of it. Therefore, instead of seeing the classics as, you know, a help—maybe even an indirect help—to get to heaven, it is, in fact, a body of literature that's valuable for its own sake.

Here's the main idea I want to focus on and that is that what we begin to have developing in the Renaissance is that there is an autonomous realm of ethics in the world. I can read the classics because I enjoy them and because they make me a little bit happier here and now, and that's sufficient. It isn't all they might do for me, I've said that before, but it's sufficient. That's a good enough reason for reading Cicero because Cicero can make me a better public speaker, a better friend, a better citizen, a better letter writer—remember, Florentines of the elite class were on the move a lot. They travel outside of Italy, as well as within Italy, working for the various banks, serving as diplomats. Machiavelli went to France. Machiavelli went to the Holy Roman Empire in, what we would call, Germany today, writing letters, writing reports. If you're working for the government or for a business, it's a very important part of that. Cicero and the other Latin writers give me a way to better do that. Cicero for executives, Cicero for government officials, and so on. And so, what's argued is not—again, I can't say this enough because it's important for us when we're looking at Machiavelli—but it's not that you dismiss the Christian or religious value of these classics, but you say they have a value in and of themselves, that is at least in principle, divorceable from that. There is an autonomous realm of living and acting and being thoughtful about moral choices that is not in and of itself simply aimed toward heaven, but it works in the here and now.

As I said, this not only leads to an intense new reading of Latin classics that have been around and finding a few new pieces here and there, it led to a new desire for Greek writing. And so, we find the study of Greek in Florence and big break—in 1453, the Byzantine Empire in Constantinople falls to the Turks and a lot of Christian writers, intellectuals, church officials, leave Constantinople and come to the West. In particular, they come to Italy, sometimes bringing their books, but also bringing their knowledge of Greek with them. There are situations we know of in Florence where a group of merchants would get together on an evening with a Greek who had emigrated from the Byzantine Empire who could teach them Greek, and they would sit and read a Greek text together. And so, we have the rediscovery of so many Greek works, the works of Plato, and one I want to focus on for just a second—the writing of Thucydides.

The History of the Peloponnesian War today has the sort of reputation of being the best damned history book ever written—and I would agree with that, by the way. He's at the top of my list of the world's greatest historical thinkers. I've always wondered, I sure wish Dante would have had Thucydides around because he could have found some really neat inhabitants of hell in there, but he didn't have

Thucydides around. But, Thucydides not only comes to the West, but he is translated into Latin in the early 15th century and so there's a whole body of political material, stories, and analysis, that Machiavelli will make use of. Machiavelli, by the way, never learned Greek, but he did have a lot of the Greek classics—works of Plato, Thucydides in Latin—and, therefore, he had a bigger view of antiquity than somebody living a century earlier who would not have known Greek and would not have had those texts available. Remember, too, that along comes the printing press in the middle of the 15th century and one of the things that means is that with the printing press—this is really cool, right—you can have books that are fairly inexpensive in Latin. In fact, as I'll talk about in the next lecture, one of the things we will discover is that Machiavelli's dad had a copy of the first ten books of Livy, printed copy. He got it for free; he probably couldn't have afforded it, because he did the index. That's sort of sitting around the Machiavelli household when little Niccolò is growing up.

Let me make one more point about Renaissance Humanist thought. We very often divide it into two periods and categories; the first period, roughly the first half of the 15th century, we refer to as civic Humanism. That is to say, we talk about the fact the classics are seen primarily as they apply to political and social life; they are practical, useful, and applicable. But, in the second half of the 15th century, there is a movement, in some sense, in a different direction symbolized by the fact that Lorenzo de Medici—again, he ruled from 1469–1492—Lorenzo de Medici founded a Platonic academy in Florence. That suggests, therefore, more of a philosophical and contemplative interest in the classics. So, we talk about a shift from civic Humanism to a more contemplative, philosophical Humanism that takes place in institutions like the Platonic Academy in Florence. However—and this is the key point I want to make at the end—Machiavelli, although he lives at the end of the 15th and in the 16th century—really is much more a civic humanist. He's not a guy who wants to sit around and talk about ideas in Plato. He's a guy who wants to take Livy and Cicero and these others and say, "How can they inform us about the way the world really works? How can they teach us things to avoid? How can they give us guidelines to help us do better by contrasting their successes with our failures?" And so, in many ways, although a little bit out of time, Machiavelli can be classified as a civic humanist. And with that, we are ready to turn next to the biography of Niccolò Machiavelli.

Lecture Four
The Life of Niccolò Machiavelli

Scope:

Machiavelli was born the year that Lorenzo de'Medici became the leader of Florence (1469) and died the year the Medici were exiled from Florence for the second time (1527). In the republican interlude between the Medici domination (1494–1512), Machiavelli led an active life as a part of Florence's government. His most important writings were produced in the years after the Medici reestablished their rulership of Florence.

However, in this lecture we shall be concerned with more than Machiavelli's career. I will present what we know about Machiavelli the man and why these personal elements are important when we analyze Machiavelli the thinker. Maybe we can come to some conclusion about why, in the most well-known portrait of Machiavelli, he has a smile as mysterious—though not as alluring—as another Florentine, Mona Lisa.

Outline

I. Niccolò Machiavelli was a member of a less distinguished branch of an old family of Florence.

   A. In the year of his birth, 1469, Lorenzo de'Medici became the de facto ruler of Florence and ruled until Machiavelli was 23 years old.

   B. We do not know much about Machiavelli's early life, though it is significant that his father obtained a printed copy of Livy's history of Rome in return for compiling the index.

   C. Machiavelli received a good education in Latin and the classics, and throughout his life, he studied and deeply admired the classics.

   D. Among "modern" writers, his clear preference was for his fellow Florentine Dante.

   E. We do not know if he saw the violent aftermath of the Pazzi conspiracy in 1478, but he must have heard many stories, because this event is mentioned often in his writings.

II. The Medici fell in 1494, and Florence returned to a republican form of government.

A. Machiavelli experienced the humiliation of the entry of the king of France into Florence.

B. It is clear from Machiavelli's writings that he listened to the sermons of Savonarola and admired him in some ways, but he was never a follower of the great preacher.

C. Just a few days after Savonarola's execution in 1498, Machiavelli received his appointment as secretary of the Second Chancery, which dealt with the territories of the Florentine Republic and foreign affairs.

III. From 1498 until 1512, Machiavelli served the government of Florence.

A. Machiavelli kept the government informed about military matters.

B. He soon began to be part of Florentine delegations to other Italian states.

    1. These included missions to Cesare Borgia, the son of Pope Alexander VI.

    2. He was present when Cesare Borgia's power crumbled after the death of his father, Alexander VI.

C. Beginning in 1500, Machiavelli also participated in diplomatic missions beyond the Alps and met with both King Louis XII of France and the Holy Roman Emperor Maximilian.

D. During these years, Machiavelli married, although for the rest of his life, he had a series of sexual liaisons with prostitutes and mistresses.

E. We have reports and other works that Machiavelli composed during his years in office.

F. From these years, and until the end of his life, Machiavelli wrote letters that have survived and give insights into his life and thought.

G. Machiavelli saw the problems of any nation relying on mercenary troops and advocated for a citizen army for Florence.

    1. He realized that in better days, Florence had had a citizen army.

    2. He recruited a citizen army that had some successes, as well as serious defects.

    3. He received a second position in government that focused on the military.

H. A disastrous defeat of the Florentines in 1512, resulting in 4,000 deaths at the nearby city of Prato, led to the end of the Florentine Republic.

IV. With the return of the Medici in 1512, Machiavelli lost his job and left Florence.

  A. He was arrested and even briefly tortured.

  B. Although he could have stayed in Florence, he would have been without any political power or voice.

    1. There was a family farm—the home was called Albergaccio—just south of Florence at Sant' Andrea in Percussina.

    2. Machiavelli chose to move there and live in a kind of voluntary retirement, although he traveled frequently to Florence.

  C. In the country, he did much business connected with the farm.

  D. He also read and studied.

  E. His life at Sant' Andrea is described in his most famous letter, written to a friend in Rome.

  F. It was at his home in the country that Machiavelli wrote *The Prince* in 1513 and the *Discourses* over the course of the next several years.

  G. He became involved with a circle of Humanists in Florence, which met in the gardens of a palazzo belonging to Bernardo Rucellai, and he wrote three plays, the most famous of which is *La Mandragola* (*The Mandrake*).

  H. He composed a life of the 14th-century *condottiere* (military leader) from Lucca, Castruccio Castracani, a Humanist portrait of a great prince.

    1. This work served perhaps as an audition to Cardinal Giulio de'Medici.

    2. The cardinal, later elected as Pope Clement VII, commissioned Machiavelli to write a history of Florence.

I. While writing this history, Machiavelli published *The Art of War*, his only political work to be published in his lifetime.

V. Machiavelli's last year was spent trying to return to political office and influence.

   A. Machiavelli was given a job concerning Florence's defense in 1526.

   B. The sack of Rome in 1527—a Medici was pope—led to the downfall of the Medici in Florence and the reestablishment of a republic.

   C. Machiavelli hoped to get his old job again, but he was ignored, perhaps because he had been too cozy with the Medici.

   D. Machiavelli died in June of 1527 and was buried in the Franciscan church of Santa Croce, where his body remains today.

Recommended Readings:

Quentin Skinner, *Machiavelli: A Very Short Introduction*.

Maurizio Viroli, *Niccolò's Smile: A Biography of Machiavelli*.

Questions to Consider:

1. Although Machiavelli wrote his most important works after his active career in politics was over, why is it vital for readers to know that he was an official of the Florentine Republic?

2. In what ways was the year 1512 pivotal in the life of Machiavelli?

3. Could Machiavelli have written the sorts of books he wrote if he had remained a "player" in Florentine politics?

Lecture Four—Transcript
The Life of Niccolò Machiavelli

If one goes back and looks in some of the late medieval or early Renaissance, depending on your periodization chronicles, one will find the name Machiavelli. That is to say, it's an old Florentine family; you find them in tax records and political lists and all the rest of it. But, it's fair to say that Niccolò Machiavelli did not come from the more distinguished or prosperous branch of the Machiavelli family. Just like there were some not very wealthy Medici running around Florence, even in the 15th century, Machiavelli was from a lesser branch of a well-known Florentine family.

He was born in the year 1469; again, this is an important year in Florentine history because it marks the year when Piero de' Medici dies and Lorenzo, called Lorenzo the Magnificent, becomes the de facto ruler of Florence. For the first 23 years of Machiavelli's life, that is what most people look back on today as the heyday of Florence. It is the time when great things, politically, are happening. Florence is relatively at peace during this period. Cosimo de Medici, the grandfather of Lorenzo, had negotiated or been a major negotiator in a kind of Italy-wide deal in 1454 called the Peace of Lodi—sometimes called Lodi, but "Lodi" would be the Italian pronunciation—where the five major states on the Italian peninsula sort of agreed to a framework where they could live with each other in relative peace. Those five, by the way, are Venice, Milan, Florence, the Papal State, and the King of Sicily who is located in Naples. Okay, the Island of Sicily is a different political entity and sort of out of it, if you will, with regard to the politics we're going to talk about.

So, Machiavelli not only grew up in a place that was culturally flourishing, Michelangelo was six years his junior, Fra Angelico was painting away, Botticelli was roughly a contemporary—a little bit older contemporary—of Machiavelli. But, he also grew up in a time of both Florentine stability and, relatively speaking, Italian stability. It's important to remember that in his own life he saw a great change from a kind of order to a kind of chaos and, clearly, that got inside his soul. He became fanatically interested in his political career and in his writing that occurred mostly after his political career ended to find some way so that Italy could prosper, and be relatively orderly and peaceful. We know very little about the childhood of Machiavelli. One of the details we know—I've mentioned it before, but it's an important detail—and that is his dad did the index to an edition, in Latin, of Livy the great Roman historian, and part of the payment for the index was a copy of the book. It was an early printed book. We need to remember early printed books were still expensive, not as expensive as manuscripts, but it wasn't really until the early 16th century that printing radically lowered the price of published material. And so, a family wouldn't have owned very many books but we now that one of the books is the Casa Machiavelli was Livy's *Early History of Rome*. And of course, that's an essentially important detail because, again, as I'm going to argue, the most important work intellectually of Niccolò Machiavelli was a commentary or *Discourses on the First Ten Books* of Livy.

We know that Machiavelli received a good education in Latin and that he has a great familiarity in his writing with the Latin classics. He did not learn Greek, but again, he wouldn't have had to read Thucydides or Plato. He wasn't one of the intellectual elites who had Greek, but he had a good knowledge of Latin and, therefore, could read what he wanted to read both from Roman and Greek antiquity. He did also read what we might call modern writers. He liked Petrarch and, in fact, he quotes Petrarch, but his real love was Dante Alighieri. He talks about, in his letters reading Dante, he quotes from Dante's *Divine Comedy*; he was a lover of that great Florentine poet who was among other things, we need to remember, a very political poet.

Although Florence was relatively peaceful and the Medici had a pretty firm grip on matters while Machiavelli was growing up, we don't want to forget, as I've mentioned before and will mention several times more, the great event of 1478, the so-called Pazzi Conspiracy—an attempt to kill Lorenzo de Medici and his brother Giuliano. His brother Giuliano was murdered in the cathedral of Florence. Lorenzo de Medici fled in safety to the sacristy and his survival led to a very quick retaliation by Florentines against those who had participated in the Pazzi Conspiracy, including the archbishop of Pisa who was hanged outside on the tower of the city hall. Now, Machiavelli's nine.

I think sometimes when we're doing history we can be too highfalutin. I try to think back about when I was nine. I was nine in the first year of the Eisenhower administration and I can remember several things that did, in fact, impact me, none of which is probably as dramatic and immediate as the Pazzi Conspiracy. I can remember the end of the Korean War because I was afraid my dad was going to go fight after he fought in World War II. And, I remember that Vice President Nixon came to my hometown to dedicate a hospital. The first time somebody in my lifetime of that level of power had been in my hometown. I didn't see him in person; I watched him on a local T.V. cut away in 1953. So, we all know, if we think about our own experiences, how first of all we remember things from when we were nine, but secondly we remember them, in part, because people talked about them around the dinner table or driving me to Little League practice for years afterward. The Korean War didn't go away in conversation around the dinner table when I was nine or ten years old, it continued for a long time. So, we need to appreciate the fact that Machiavelli witnessed this attempt to eliminate the Medici and he witnessed the response of the Florentines to it. Whether this is what got him interested in politics, we might say today, we don't know. But, certainly, he writes a lot about the Pazzi Conspiracy in various works of his.

In 1494, Machiavelli is now 25 years old. The French invade Italy. The Florentine leader, Lorenzo's son Piero, handles it badly and is forced into exile and Florence once again returns to a more clear and direct republican form of government. Remember that the Florentines always used the word republic to describe Florence, but really the Medici dominated Florentine politics for 60 years. Now, there's sort of a fresh start, constitutionally, with new figures that come to the fore in the absence of the Medici and with the presence in Italy of the French and not too long thereafter, German, Swiss, and Spanish as well. We certainly must expect that Machiavelli would have heard the sermons of the great preacher Savonarola. He preached not only in his own church, San Marco, but he also preached in the cathedral and he was a dominant figure in leading Florence toward a certain kind of republican government. And, when Machiavelli writes about Savonarola, he writes about him respectfully. Although, certainly, he was never caught up in Savonarola's ultimately apocalyptic fervor or his burning of the wigs and the paintings and all the other vanities that he called for in various bonfires. No doubt, Machiavelli was in Florence when Savonarola's life came to an end. When, ultimately, Savonarola would not obey Papal orders, he was tried, convicted, and executed in the main square of Florence in May of 1498.

So, all of these stories that we hear about in our textbooks, we see in films about the Renaissance; they're part of the lived experience of Machiavelli. By the time he's 25 years old, he could remember the best days of Lorenzo de Medici. He can remember the unveiling of great works of art. He can remember the Pazzi Conspiracy. He can remember what would have been seen, even then, as the tragedy of the death of Lorenzo de Medici. The incompetence of Piero, the invasion of the French, the preaching of Savonarola, the burning of Savonarola—these are all things that are already in the experience of the young man Niccolò Machiavelli who was not yet 30 years old.

Just a few days after Savonarola was burned, Machiavelli received his first job with the government. He was appointed as secretary of the Second Chancery—that was his official title—and when we see pictures of him, he's usually dressed in the outfit he would have worn as an official of the Florentine republic. What did the Second Chancery do? Remembering that secretary is an important job, like today we use the term Secretary of State or whatever, he is an important official in the Second Chancery. It did two things. First of all, it dealt with the territory that belonged to Florence; it was part of the Florentine state outside the walls. That's a lot of towns, a lot of countryside to administer. Secondly, it dealt, at least somewhat, with foreign affairs, remembering that foreign affairs doesn't mean just outside of Italy. It means, first and foremost, Siena, Luca, and other neighboring independent city-states in Italy. And so, Machiavelli got his job in 1498. He held that job and later on got a second job for 14 years until the collapse of the republic in 1512. He kept the Florentine government, which was changing leaders all the time in many of the bodies that deliberated, although there was a head of government named Piero Soderini who was around the whole time. He informed the government about military matters and he seemed to have made enough of an impression that he began doing diplomatic missions.

One that clearly affected him for the rest of his life was the fact that he was in the presence, on more than one occasion, of Cesare Borgia, the son of Pope Alexander the VI. Popes had sons back in those days and admitted it we need to remember, Alexander the VI, member of the Borgia family, had, you may recall a son and a daughter Lucrezia. And, much of the pontificate of Alexander the VI dealt with finding Cesare some land and Lucrezia a husband; neither one came easily for Alexander the VI, as it turned out. He was with Cesare Borgia, in fact, when Alexander the VI died. That happened at a time when Cesare was ill and, therefore, despite the fact that he admired Cesare Borgia, he saw the way Cesare Borgia took a piece of land, got control of it, and brought order to it. He'll talk about that a lot in *The Prince* and we'll look at those passages in great detail. But, he also saw the end of Cesare Borgia's career when, if you will, the wrong guy was elected Pope to succeed Alexander the VI, the member of the Borgia family who was Cesare's father, and Cesare's little empire in Italy collapsed. So, he witnesses the best and the worst of Cesare Borgia. This gives him a real sense of Italian politics, and what's going on in Italy, and how things worked, and how diplomacy worked, and what kinds of activities worked because Cesare is an important kind of prince. He did not inherit any land; he took what he ruled. The question is if you do that, if you acquire a principality, how do you run it? How do you get it organized? How do you get respect? How do you maintain power? And, of course, those are going to be principal issues in *The Prince* because *The Prince* is not entirely but largely about those princes who acquire new territories. Cesare is the single most important model that he has.

Beginning in 1500—he's only been on the job a couple years now, this Machiavelli guy —beginning in 1500, Machiavelli began to participate in diplomatic missions to France and to the Holy Roman Empire. In fact, that meant he traveled outside of Italy. He was in the presence of both the King of France and the Holy Roman Emperor, and he got what today we would think of as greater international exposure—although, technically, again, Italy's a bunch of countries. Getting outside of Italy clearly gave him a much broader perspective and he will not just be able to compare one Italian city-state with another or the ancient Roman Republic with one Italian city-state, but he will also be able to talk about German free cities. He'll be able to talk about the King of France. Therefore, his bag of modern examples and illustrations is much more filled than it would have been had he simply remained a figure that was involved doing things in Italy.

During the years when Machiavelli was working for the Florentine government, like all, or like virtually all, young men who did not go into the clergy, Machiavelli married. How do we say this nicely? Machiavelli wasn't real big on keeping his wedding vows. There was, it seems, an endless and open group of mistresses and prostitutes that he tells about, sometimes in quite vulgar detail, sort of more than you want to know, about what happens in the basement of some dive, some place or other where Machiavelli has gone. Machiavelli began to write during his years as an employee, as an official of the Florentine government. Some of those things are simply government reports, but he also began to write other works, as well. Also in these years, Machiavelli began to write letters. I emphasized this in the first lecture and I'm going to read from one of his later ones in this lecture. The letters provide us a much richer sense of who this man is, how he's living his life, how his thought is developing, and so this great treasure trove of letters really begins not from the period when he's writing the famous works *The Prince* and *The Discourses* and whatever, but when he is a Florentine republican official.

Now, Machiavelli looked around and he said, "What are the problems we, in the Florentine republic, have to solve?" There are obviously all the diplomatic problems dealing with other countries, but one that Machiavelli saw that became—it's probably fair to say—an obsession is that Florence needed a citizen army. Florence, like other city-states, even in the 13th century and especially in the 14th and 15th century, more and more relied on mercenaries. It relied not on individuals, but paid companies, bought companies of soldiers, usually under the leadership of some minor noble in Italy who's out to make a fortune and perhaps even capture a territory to rule. Machiavelli knew enough Florentine history to know that in the good old days a long time ago, when Florence was more successful than it was in his own day militarily, Florence had a citizen army. And so, he began as an official of the republic to recruit a citizen army. Let me just say that that citizen army had a mixed record in the last years of the Florentine republic. It had some modest successes; it had some very serious defects. But, this was important enough to enough people that Machiavelli was actually given a second job where he was sort of put in charge of organizing a militia among Florentines within the Florentine republic. So, he becomes not just a diplomatic guy, but also a military guy.

Then, in 1512, it all fell part after a defeat of the Florentines resulted in a slaughter of 4,000 people in the nearby city of Prato, which was part of the Florentine republic. The republic collapsed and the Medici returned in 1512. With the return of the Medici, Machiavelli was fired. He was so identified with the republican regime that he was simply dismissed from office. In fact, Machiavelli was briefly arrested and even tortured. That didn't last very long and he could have continued to live in Florence, but he chose not to. Perhaps you'd be a little bit squeamish if you think, "Gosh, they might change their mind and get into this torture stuff again." But, at any rate, Machiavelli chose to live on the family farm south of Florence. He commuted into Florence a lot. This family farm is in a tiny, and I mean a *tiny*, village called Sant' Andrea in Percussina, in a house called the Albergaccio. That's where Machiavelli lived, really on and off, the rest of his life.

Now, I went there this summer; it is really in the boonies. It's about 12 kilometers of Florence, but you'd swear to God you know there were only olive trees and vineyards. In fact, today they sell olive oil and wine made from plants on the Machiavelli estate. But what's interesting, from the backyard of a modest villa, one can actually see the dome of the cathedral of Florence, probably clearer then than now because of pollution. I remember standing there and just sort of wondering, boy, just every day of his life, you sort of picture him standing there and saying, "Damn, I wish I were there. I wish I were in all the hustle and bustle. I wish I were going off to my job in the government and really wheeling and dealing and making things better, and here I am on this farm and I just sort of need to stay here and this is the place that I operate out of." So, this kind of voluntary retirement took place in Sant' Andrea in Percussina.

Now, what did he do there? Well, Machiavelli's not a rich guy and so he had to manage the estate while he was there, and some of the letters that he writes during this early period, especially at Sant' Andrea, are really quite funny. He's got to go sell some birds, and he's got to make sure that Jacomo the farmer, or whoever it is, is taking care of things he's supposed to be taking care of. And well, there's an inn right across the street. You go there and you have a glass of wine and you play cards and other games, and you talk about trivia with all these sort of brutish guys who work out in the country. I'm not using my language now; I'm sort of paraphrasing Machiavelli. And, he finds himself occupied in the day with things that he regards as trivial because this guy really is a political animal. He wants to be where the action is and the action is not selling thrushes so somebody can have thrush dinner. That's not what Machiavelli wants to do. But, again, it's safer there and in one of his most famous letters he writes to his friend Francesco Vettori in Rome, he says there was another side.

Let me read you this passage, probably the most famous passage from all of Machiavelli's letters: "When evening comes, I return to my home and I go into my study and on the threshold I take off my everyday clothes, which are covered with mud and mire and I put on regal imperial robes and dressed in a more appropriate manner, I enter into the ancient courts of ancient men. And am welcomed by them kindly. And there I taste the food that alone is mine and for which I was born. And there I am not ashamed to speak to them. I ask them the reasons for their actions and they in their humanity answer me. And for four hours I feel no boredom. I dismiss every affliction. I no longer fear poverty nor do I tremble at the thought of death." Machiavelli says, "I go in my library. I change clothes and I get out these ancient books. I read Livy. I read Cicero. I read these other works." And notice—remember I said that in the mid-14th century that Petrarch writes a letter to Cicero. Notice what Machiavelli says, "I converse with these great authors. I ask them questions and they answer me."

This is part of the great genius of Niccolò Machiavelli. I think we all understand something of what he's getting at because when you read old books seriously, and you're not merely an antiquarian, you're asking those authors questions, sometimes questions they couldn't have directly imagined because you ask them a question that comes out of your experience individually or politically. We all know, we'd like to ask the great thinkers of the past, well what would you do today if you were around and problem X was in front of you? And, an intelligent reading of those classics tries to say I'm going to try to find the answer, I'm not going to make it up. I'm not going to say, "This is what I want Cicero to say and, therefore, this is what Cicero says." You have to read these books carefully. You've got to not have them simply say what you'd like them to say, but really to answer based on your careful reading of what their principles were, what their method of argumentation was, what their kind of evidence was, and how they used evidence to draw conclusions about their own day or about their own past.

When I walked into that room—it's not a museum, I was able to get in there—when you walk into that room, there's still a desk where Machiavelli would be. And, it isn't a very big room, but one pictures him putting on that robe, taking off the farmer's clothes, and one pictures him with a big book—because books tended to be bigger in those days. Not very many books, there wouldn't have been shelves lined with books like we think of as a library today, but taking down a copy of Livy, or a copy of Cicero, or a copy of Thucydides, and sitting there and talking to those folks. Not literally, but really asking them questions, not as an antiquarian, "Now, exactly, where did that soldier move in 434 B.C. when he did this?" Not that, but rather asking him broader questions, finding ways to apply ancient understanding, ancient wisdom, ancient experience, including ancient experience gone wrong, to his own life and to the situation of his own life. And so, it was there, in that room, in fact, that he wrote *The Prince* and that he wrote *The Discourses on Livy* over the next several years. That's the context. That removal from the everyday and that withdrawal into a more pure kind of thought that he could have had, were he a government official where he's also got to write a report for tomorrow or deal with some damn diplomat from Siena tomorrow; he didn't have to do that. He really is able to be with those great authors.

He also began to go into Florence to become associated with the humanist circle, some people who would get together in the garden of a villa of the Rucellai family and they would read classical text together. They read not just historical or philosophical text, but all kinds of literature and that's probably the origin of him writing three plays. *The Mandrake Root, La Mandragola,* is the most famous of the plays that Machiavelli wrote. We don't often think of him as a playwright. They're pretty funny. In occasion, they're pretty dirty. But, Machiavelli grew into that sort of larger sense of the humanities, not only the political text. But still—bottom line—he was a political animal. He wrote a biography of Castruccio Castracani, a 14th-century military leader from Luca, and many think it was a kind of application to the Medici. If that's true, it was successful because Cardinal Julio de Medici commissioned Machiavelli to write a history of Florence. By the way, Julio de Medici shortly after that time was elected as Pope Clement VII and, therefore, by the time it was finished, it was the work that had been commissioned by the bishop of Rome, the Pope.

While writing it, this history of Florence, Machiavelli also wrote a book called *The Art of War.* It was the only political work published in his own lifetime. Machiavelli wanted to get back into office. He wanted to be a player in Florentine politics again. In addition to writing a history for the Medici, he was indeed, in 1526, given a fairly minor job concerning the defense and the defensive structures for the city of Florence. But in 1527, the Holy Roman Emperor sacked Rome, weakening the Pope—who was a Medici, remember—and the weakening of the Medici in Rome led to the expulsion of the Medici from Florence, early in 1527. This is one of those good news-bad news situations for Machiavelli. It's good news because there can be a republic again. It's bad news because, well, in recent years the Medici had actually commissioned him to do some things. Machiavelli hoped to get his old job back and didn't probably, as I mentioned earlier, because in the eyes of the people putting together the new government, he was too associated with the Medici—what an irony.

He died in June of 1527 and was immediately buried in the Franciscan church of Santa Croce, a church that also contains the bodies of Michelangelo and Galileo. So, Machiavelli dies just as the republic was forming again. That's now the background; we have some history of Florence, we have some history of Humanist thought, and we have a biography of Machiavelli. Roll up your sleeves because we're ready to go to *The Prince* and start our process of reading that extraordinarily important work.

Lecture Five
Why Did Machiavelli Write *The Prince*?

Scope:

We know a great deal about the circumstances in which Machiavelli wrote what has become his most famous work, *The Prince*. Although much of that knowledge comes from *The Prince* itself, we also have letters that Machiavelli wrote from his country estate, where he composed that powerful little book.

In studying *The Prince*, we also come to realize that, although Machiavelli owes a great deal to classical writers from whom he borrowed examples and ideas, he is quite original in his thoughts and theories, disagreeing with both Aristotle and Cicero.

Outline

I. When Machiavelli "retired" to his farm in Sant' Andrea in Percussina, he kept abreast of politics and longed to return an active political life.

    A. He engaged in farm work, but he also continued to study history.

    B. This fact is clearest from a letter he wrote to his friend Francesco Vettori in Rome.

II. In 1513, during his first months in the country, Machiavelli composed *The Prince* and sent it to Vettori to show to the Medici.

    A. A traditional argument is that *The Prince* is something of a work of flattery and, indirectly, a job application to the Medici.

    B. It is important to note that the basic form of *The Prince* is an example of a popular genre of treatises of advice to princes, sometimes referred to as *mirrors of princes*.

    C. Recently, Princeton professor Maurizio Viroli suggested that *The Prince*, far from being a work of flattery, is deeply critical of traditional Medici ways of governing and, thus, suggests that the returning Medici must govern differently to be successful.

III. Machiavelli is deeply indebted to many classical writers for ideas and examples in *The Prince*.

    A. Machiavelli also provides many examples from his own time, some of which he directly experienced in his capacity as an official of the Florentine Republic.

    B. Typically of Humanist writers, he cites no examples from the period we call the Middle Ages.

        1. We thus see, in Machiavelli, a view of a brilliant ancient culture, followed by a long period of insignificance, followed by a time in which there is a partial restoration of classical values.

        2. Machiavelli is interested in the role of the Church as a political power in Italy, but he is apparently totally disinterested in theology and religious arguments concerning political power and arrangements.

IV. Machiavelli's *The Prince* is stunningly original and is neither a repetition of any classical writer nor a synthesis of classical works.

    A. Machiavelli disagrees with the great Greek political philosopher Aristotle.

        1. For Aristotle, the state is founded on friendship and trust, while for Machiavelli, it is based on the fear of the prince and a system of coercion.

        2. Aristotle sees the study of politics as an empirical science but seeks to find what ought to be, while Machiavelli sees politics as the science of what is.

    B. One can read *The Prince* as a systematic refutation of the political views of Cicero, regarded by Humanists as the greatest of all the Roman sages.

        1. Cicero argued that political leaders must exercise the standard virtues, such as honesty and magnanimity.

        2. Cicero believed that rulers must be loved and that fear is insufficient to sustain power.

        3. Machiavelli argues that a prince must be prepared to act immorally—lying and deceiving and exercising cruelty.

        4. Machiavelli recognizes the value to the prince of his subjects' fear of him.

        5. Machiavelli believes that a prince's first priority is the maintenance of the state and that a prince must be flexible—even immoral, cruel, and deceptive—in the means he uses.

6. Machiavelli is arguing for a distinction between personal and political morality.

   a. What makes a man a saint or a good father or husband will often be disastrous when applied by a prince in political matters.

   b. There was a movement during the Renaissance to suggest an autonomous morality in the world, but Machiavelli carries this idea beyond his Humanist predecessors.

   c. Because of this, Machiavelli has been referred to as "the first modern man," although that idea is probably not very useful for us in understanding the totality of his thought.

Recommended Readings:

Maurizio Viroli, "Introduction," in Machiavelli's *The Prince*, translated by Peter Bondanella, pp. vii–xxxix.

Questions to Consider:

1. Can we determine why Machiavelli wrote *The Prince* and what he hoped to gain from writing it?

2. Given how "realistic" and hard-nosed *The Prince* is, how do we fit that with the fact that Machiavelli wrote it while engaged in a rather solitary study of ancient authors?

3. What is the essence of Machiavelli's new political morality?

Lecture Five—Transcript
Why Did Machiavelli Write *The Prince*?

Now, we're going to begin our course within a course. We're going to begin to look at Machiavelli's *The Prince*, a short work, but certainly his most famous work—the work from which the Machiavellian adjective comes. Machiavelli, again, retired from his active political work in 1512. Of course, it was—as I pointed out in the biographical lecture—a forced retirement. Florence, we would say today, changed governments and he was out. Furthermore, as I also pointed out in the last lecture, he was not only out of office, he decided it was probably in his better interests and probably good for his health to actually leave Florence and go live a few kilometers south of Florence in the countryside on the old Machiavelli estate—a rather modest villa by the standards of what we think of today when we think of a Renaissance villa. Nevertheless, it was not a bad place to live in the country.

However, Machiavelli's forced retirement hardly kept him from being interested in and informed about politics in Florence. He really kept track of things; again, he was free to go into the city when he wanted to and he could literally see the city from his backyard. Also, he had a lot of news, he wrote letters, he corresponded with people not just in the immediate area, but also in Rome and so on. Let's put it this way, if Machiavelli were living in 2005 and had the same situation, we would say that he'd probably become a C-SPAN junkie. He really wanted to know what was going on in the politics. It was in his blood. Florence was in his blood and so he kept track of things, but what's really interesting is that while he was eager to get back to work, eager to get back into politics, we would say, he also had time to read, to contemplate, to think. At least I imagine Machiavelli, as he's walking from one place on the farm to the other, not really pondering, gosh, how are the hogs doing today, but really pondering if I'd had done this differently or if King Louis' troops do this, or if such and such happens, or if the Pope dies or whatever it might be, then what are going to be the political fallouts from all of that sort of stuff. So, Machiavelli was both almost still feverish in his interest in politics and yet somewhat contemplative, and it was during these first months of his enforced retirement and his voluntary exile from the city of Florence that he, indeed, wrote *The Prince*. It was done by Christmas of 1513.

I read to you, in the last lecture, part of a letter that Machiavelli wrote to his friend Francesco Vettori in Rome, sort of describing daily life, but also, in particular, describing his study and describing his writing, as he was working in his little village of Sant' Andrea in Percussina. Now, he wrote *The Prince* quickly—in a matter of months—and a good question to ask is, well, why? What kind of a book is it? What was the purpose? What was he going to get out of it? What was the function of that work, as he understood it, as he was writing it? Since he did, after all, send it on to Rome—and remember, Rome is important because there is a Medici pope in Rome. Leo X is the Pope and, therefore, when he sends it to Rome, he is sending it to a seat of Medici power. In fact, this is a very important point to make. Remember earlier I mentioned there are five principal politic powers in Italy, but that Italy was also subject to these foreign invasions beginning in 1494. Well, Machiavelli is really put off by the arrival of the French and the Spanish and all the rest of them and wants the—as he calls them in *The Prince*—the barbarians out of Italy.

But, there's a fortuitous series of events that's occurred, as Machiavelli sees it, because now at this moment, two of those five principal powers in Italy are held by the same family. That is to say, the Medici have to come back to power in Florence and there is a Medici on the papal throne, on the Throne of St. Peter. Therefore, Machiavelli no doubt sees this as an opportunity that perhaps now he can see the Medici are the family that really need to take charge in Italy. That they're the ones because of this fortuitous situation, the Medici return in Florence and the election of Leo X as Pope, that together the Medici can be the leaders of the Italians to, among other things, bring some law and order in Italy and throw out the barbarians, the foreign troops and invaders. And so, one way people have traditionally read Machiavelli's *The Prince* is as a kind of work of flattery, and even as a job application to the Medici. Because, even though the Medici replaced the republican government where Machiavelli had been an official, Machiavelli was a Florentine and he wanted to go to work for the new government, although he was somewhat distrusted because of his identification with the previous regime.

And so, many see this as, "Hey, Medici, first of all, let me tell you, I love you guys." Certainly, at the very beginning and the very end of *The Prince*—and we'll talk about those pieces in detail at the appropriate time—certainly, there's this sense of a little bit of flattery of the Medici. For example, although originally this was dedicated to a member of the Medici family who died very shortly after it was written, the dedication as it reads today is to Lorenzo de' Medici—not the one who died, of course, in 1492. The Medici kept naming their kids the same things, it gets sort of confusing, but this is another Lorenzo de' Medici whom he calls in the dedicatory letter, "The magnificent." Well, there wasn't much magnificent about this particular Lorenzo de' Medici and so one sometimes sees it as a work of flattery and as a job application: "This is what I think, this is how I would advise you, hire me, hire me, hire me."

That's one way to read what *The Prince* is. Let me suggest two other ways, however, that we can read *The Prince*. One is we're stunned by its newness. When we read this book, especially in a college "great books" course or wherever it might be, we think of it as something that just seems to come out of nowhere. There's never been a book like this before. Again, it's led to such titles that we give Machiavelli as "The first modern man." Well, let me suggest that that's true and not true. Let me talk about the way it's not true because it's true in obvious ways. For centuries, indeed for a millennium and a half, one can argue there has been a genre of literature called a mirror for princes. Primarily, this was a medieval genre of literature, although it has been argued that the earliest one of these dates from around 400 B.C. and was written by the Greek Xenophon. That is to say, they are books of advice, books for princes to hold up as mirrors in their hands and look at themselves and examine themselves carefully, as you can do when you look in a good mirror. And so, in many ways, although this book is startlingly new, it is from another point of view, conventional in genre. It is simply the most famous of a whole body of literature of manuals or, again, to use the better word, mirrors of princes. I was teaching a course last semester on the early Middle Ages. We were reading a document from the 9th century and, sure enough, it's a mirror for princes written by an advisor to one of the successors of Charlemagne. So, it is important to say that although this is, in some ways, perhaps a job application, perhaps even a flattering job application, it is also from a traditional genre of literature—advice to, mirrors for, princes.

In recent years, one of the great scholars of Machiavelli today, Maurizio Viroli, who teaches at Princeton, has written that, in fact, this is not a very flattering book to the Medici at all; that's a misreading of the text. In fact, what he wants to argue is, this is a book that is deeply critical of the Medici. That doesn't mean it isn't a job application. But instead of saying—"Boy, you guys are great. Boy, you guys are going to run a great regime. Boy, I'd like to work for you, you're really cool"—Viroli argues what this says is, "Look, hold this up as a mirror and you will see that my advice is very different from the way you're acting and you guys are messing things up. You guys are making big time mistakes. And,"—of course, here's the other implication—"you need me because, presumably, you aren't getting very good advice. You guys are not running things very well and you're going to perpetuate or deepen the problems of Italy, rather than solve them if you keep going the way you're going." So it may be, in fact, to attract the attention of the Medici and to show Machiavelli's own importance to the success of the Medici in Rome and in Florence. But, at least, Viroli argues, it doesn't do it in a flattering way; it does it in a witheringly critical way. And so, these are some of the ways that we can read the book as a whole.

Let me turn now to asking where does Machiavelli get his information? That is to say, there is, in addition to advice, a lot of information in this book, information in the sense of examples of how things are done right, how things are done wrong. Therefore, we need to ask, where does Machiavelli look? Where do his examples and his stories and his illustrations come from? Because it is a well illustrated book in terms of the specificity of detail, historical and contemporary. One thing it's worth saying is if we simply make a list of the proper names, who gets mentioned in *The Prince*? You would find very quickly, with almost no exceptions, that the lists really fall into two categories. Category one: ancient people, Greeks and Romans, some of whom are pretty well-known to us still today and some of whom are fairly obscure, unless you've read a lot of Thucydides and some of the other Greek and Roman authors. So, you will find Hannibal, for example; there's a big star, we know that name. We will also find a lot of what most people today would regard as fairly obscure ancient figures, although they're more obscure to us than they would be to the Humanist educated people who were likely to read *The Prince* in the first place.

The second big group of people is modern people, meaning from the 15th and early 16th century. Many of the people who Machiavelli mentions are, in fact, alive or very, very recently dead. Now, what I want you to notice is there's a gap because if you've got ancient people and, from Machiavelli's point of view, modern people, what you don't have is medieval people. That is to say, for roughly a 1,000-year period that we today call the Middle Ages—remember, I say this as a medievalist, first and foremost—there is virtually no reference. We don't have reference to, you know, some of the great kings of medieval Europe that we think of, Louis IX of France, or Richard the Lion Hearted, or Edward I, the Father of Parliament—none of those folks make it. This is basically a study that largely compares ancient people and modern people with almost nothing in-between. In many ways, that's very typical of Humanists in Florence in the 15th and 16th centuries. That is to say, it's very typical of the Renaissance. Again, the Renaissance is the period where we say stuff was born—stuff sort of died and stuff gets reborn. Well, if that's your view of things, then of course the dead period doesn't matter very much. That's not where you're going to draw the most important lessons. Those are not the writers you're going to look to for the most wisdom and so it's very interesting to see this gap because Machiavelli is one of many of those Humanists who, even without doing it in words, really creates the notion of ancient, medieval, and modern, with medieval sort of meaning barbaric and uninteresting and not very useful to us.

That Renaissance, and, later on, Enlightenment view of the Middle Ages, continued until modern times when the Middle Ages got discovered. After all, American universities had been teaching history a long time before Harvard hired the first medieval historian in the United States. By the way, that was Henry Adams, the famous 19th-century scholar and thinker and member of the Adams family. That's Adams family, of course, with one "d" and not two. So, I do want to emphasize that Machiavelli does enforce this Humanist notion that the ancient world is a treasury of examples and wisdom from the past, and the modern world is a world upon which we are playing right now, and the world in-between really isn't very interesting or valuable.

Another point that's worth making, as we begin to look at what Machiavelli talks and doesn't talk about, he obviously deals with the church a great deal. After all, in every part of Europe the church is a great landowner, a political power, the Bishop of Florence, still counts in politics. But of course, most importantly for Machiavelli, he examines the role of the Pope because the Papal States was one of the nations on the Italian peninsula, one of five that really mattered.

There were some smaller ones. Therefore, he's constantly interested in talking about the papacy as a political entity and as, in particular, a political entity governed by an official who has a spiritual job—the job of being the vicar of Christ, the bishop of Rome, and the successor of Peter. However, Machiavelli never is interested in theology. He never talks about traditional Christian teaching. Morality, Christian ethics, those concerns are not there; what the church teaches doesn't seem to be very interesting to him. He's interested in the church and religion as players in the realm of politics. He's not particularly interested in Christianity in terms of its religious belief or its ultimate goal of achieving salvation for those who adhere to the faith. It is in that way a very secular book.

It is not to say that Machiavelli is an atheist. As far as we know, he went to church on Sundays. There are certainly times when he talks about the existence of God and God directing Moses to open the Red Sea, as he retells the story of Moses from the book of Exodus. He may have a kind of conventional and general belief in God, but he is really not interested in theology, in Christian morality, Christian ethics, as a guide to politics. Therefore, although we should not call him irreligious, or perhaps even in his personal life, non-religious, religious reasoning, religious motivation really doesn't enter into this or the other books of Machiavelli at all. He's famous toward the end of his life in having written a letter to a friend of his in which he said, "I love Florence." By Florence, he not only means his country, but also all the political parts of Florence. "I love Florence," he says, "more than my own soul." I guess we could say that says something about him twice: A) what his priorities are, and B) presumably he thinks he has a soul. So, we can take his religion or lack of religion into account. We need to remember it as we read, partly because of what's not there that we might traditionally expect to be there.

Now, what I want to do for almost all the rest of this lecture is to talk about how Machiavelli specifically responds to certain classical authors and challenges, or re-does or undoes much of what Cicero and Aristotle, in particular, have written. Let's begin in chronological order—I am a historian, after all—with Aristotle, the great Greek philosopher of the 4th century B.C. Aristotle argued that the state, the nation, the government is founded on friendship and trust. That it's the basis of a community, of one of these great city-states, such as Athens where Aristotle lived, although he was not a native. If you ask what's the building block? Where do you start?

What do you need to have a state and to have it work successfully? It is that you need a certain kind of bond between citizens, a bond that we would refer to in terms of friendship and trust. That's how states work. That's how states function. That's how they become cohesive. That's how armies stand together in the field of battle. But, Machiavelli challenges this.

Machiavelli argues that the basis of the state is the fear of the prince and its system of coercion—that is to say, the laws that say do this or here's the punishment, or don't do this or here's the punishment. And so, while Aristotle really talks about a kind of personal and moral basis of the state, for Machiavelli it is much more about fear and power; that's what holds people together. It's important for us to understand that when Machiavelli makes these arguments about fear and about the coercion of law, he is in some ways challenging traditional views. You know, Aristotle, as I mentioned in an earlier lecture, unlike Plato and whatever, had come back in his writings into Western Europe in the 12th and 13th centuries. Therefore, Aristotle is already well integrated into Western thought before the Renaissance comes along. Even in 1300 or a little after, when Dante's writing *The Divine Comedy*, as I pointed out, what does he call Aristotle? He calls him, simply, the philosopher. That's how deeply rooted Aristotelian ideas are in the Western tradition. It's almost, not quite, but almost as if, if Aristotle says it, unless it is contradicted by the Bible, it must be right. That's not an unfair way to talk about the respect that Aristotle had. Machiavelli comes along and challenges that.

Now, let's talk about the way Aristotle understands, what we would today call, political science. It was, indeed, an empirical science. You went out and you got data. When Aristotle was interested in how to understand city-states, he sent out a team of researchers—what we would call the constitutional histories of all the existing Greek city-states—to see, as he drew them all together, what they have in common, what things work, what things lead to injustice, and whatever. It's an empirical science, but the goal of that science is to discover what ought to be. Let me say that again—the goal of political science, as empirical as it is, is to find out what ought to be. Let's see how all these states work and then let's see, from that, if we can say this is the way states ought to organize themselves. This is the way states ought to write laws. This is the way we ought to legislate. This is the way rulers ought to govern. It has, ultimately, a purpose of designing a kind of ideal, a model, a perfect version of what a just state is.

Of course, Machiavelli, too, is quite empirical. Again, *The Prince* and other works are full of examples, full of data we might say, taken especially from the ancient world and from contemporary times. But, Machiavelli is not doing this with the idea of saying, "Now, let's take all that we figured out, all we've gathered together, and argue how things ideally ought to work." Machiavelli's political science, if you will, is much more descriptive. "Roll up your sleeves, guys, this is the reality. This is the way the world works. This is the way that things have to go." You can't get wedded into a particular way of conduct because situations change and what works in situation A will not work in situation B; you have to shift gears. Therefore, you have to be flexible because what you're interested in, what political science is interested in, is order and power, not building some sort of model, but order and power. How things really work, how, if you are a prince, to stay a prince and by staying a prince, you've got to be able to organize the world at your governing in a way that will provide for your security and safety. And so, although there are certain similarities between Aristotelian political science and Machiavellian political science, at least in terms of gathering evidence and being empirical, the goals are quite different.

Having said that, let me now turn to Cicero. Cicero, in the 20th century, has sort of declined, I guess we would say, as somebody who really belonged in that pantheon of the greatest of classical thinkers; he just sort of dropped a notch or two. We need to remember that before the 20th century, Cicero was one of the great authorities. When Dante creates his structure of hell, for example, we find out that what he does is combine two different ideas of evil—one based on Aristotle, one based on Cicero. Today, when people read that in the footnote, they say, "Gee, Aristotle, you know, greatest philosopher ever along with Plato, but Cicero sort of a second-rater." But, we need to remember, whether that modern judgment of Cicero is right or wrong, that Cicero had the highest reputation as a rhetorician and as a thinker and he was particularly venerated during the Renaissance because he was the great republican writer. He lived at the end of the Roman republic and wrote a great deal that was about reflections on government. He even wrote a book called *On the Republic*. He wrote a book on duties. These were, primarily, right at the top of the list of the great books you would have read had you been educated in Florence when Machiavelli was. So, what I want to suggest is that one of the things that Machiavelli does in *The Prince* is he—maybe systematically is a little bit too strong, but maybe it's not—he really goes about destroying some of the basic Ciceronian precepts that really hadn't even been challenged during the Renaissance. They were simply accepted as the way things are.

Let me give you some examples. Cicero argued that political leaders must exercise, what we would call today, I suppose, the standard virtues. The four great classical virtues of, wisdom, justice, temperance, and fortitude, and they needed to be honest and magnanimous. Those are things that made you a great man. Those are things that made you a great political leader. Cicero argued that political rulers must be loved because fear was insufficient to sustain power. You can't scare people into law and order. The citizens must love their ruler if it is to be an organized and functioning and just state. So, think about those two principles; love is more important than fear and a good prince exercises, if you will, writ large, the same virtues that he exercises as an individual. To put it another way, what makes you a good friend, a good neighbor, a good dad, a good husband, whatever, also makes you a good ruler and vice versa; what makes you a bad friend would also make you a bad ruler. Therefore, there was one morality; sometimes it was writ small, sometimes it was writ large, if you will, in capital letters, but it's the same basic morality.

Machiavelli takes on those principles. He argued that a prince must be prepared to act immorally, lying, deceiving, and exercising cruelty, because not to do those things, to be sort of the boy scout leader, if you will, of a nation was a formula for disaster. It was a formula for failure, a formula for disorder. Remember, as Machiavelli looks at his own world, it is a disordered world. There are factions within city-states. The Florentine government has just changed. The barbarians are running wild in Italy. So, when Machiavelli looks and asks, "What's going to bring order and stability?" It's not Mr. Nice Guy because that doesn't work. What princes need to do, when necessary, not just gratuitously, is to lie, to deceive, and to be cruel. Machiavelli also recognizes the need for leaders to be feared. We'll talk about one of the most famous lines in *The Prince* in a future lecture where Machiavelli asks, "Is it better to be loved or to be feared?" Of course, Machiavelli's answer is, "Ideally, it's best to be both." But, that doesn't often happen, so it's better to be feared than loved. What we need to see is not that statement sort of blinking at us on the page; what we need to see is that Machiavelli is challenging an almost up-to-that-time unchallenged principle of how you govern a state.

What Machiavelli is doing, therefore, in this dismantling of Ciceronian ideas of leadership, what he's really doing, therefore, is this: He's saying that what makes a good man—or woman, but these are men who are rulers—what makes a person a saint, what makes a person a good dad, can be disastrous if that leader exercises those virtues. That there is a kind of divorce, we might say, between personal and political morality, and that a prince must be willing to do what traditionally would be called immoral things—to be cruel, to lie, to deceive, to present image rather than reality to people. In many ways, we can see this as a development, albeit not a necessary development, of what I talked about as a basic principle of the Renaissance, which is to create a kind of autonomous moral world on earth. This is a set of rules that help me live better right here on Earth, rather than seeing every rule on earth simply directed toward me getting to heaven. Therefore, Machiavelli is taking that Renaissance idea and applying it in a way that it had never been applied before. There's also an autonomous morality, if you will, that exists for rulers, above and beyond, and different from and often in opposition to, all of the personal morality. Very often, it is for that reason that Machiavelli is referred to as the first modern man.

Lecture Six
The Prince, 1–5—Republics Old and New

Scope:

If we are going to understand *The Prince*, we need to take seriously its author's words. Hence, in this and the following five lectures, we will be "text crawling."

First, we will need to consider the original and revised dedications of the book—both to members of the Medici family. We will also consider how this work can be seen as an attempt to win the favor of the Medici so that Machiavelli could return to Florence and be of service to his beloved city.

The first few chapters are often passed over rather quickly, for they are something of a catalogue of types of principalities and ways that they acquire new territory.

Chapter 4 is Machiavelli's first extended use of examples from classical antiquity to illuminate his discussion. He also makes use of the examples of the Ottoman Empire and France in his own time. We will discuss this chapter both for Machiavelli's appeal to the past and the focus of *The Prince* on the present.

Outline

I. The dedication of *The Prince* in the earliest printed copies that exist is to Lorenzo de'Medici, Duke of Urbino (not, of course, the Lorenzo de'Medici who had ruled Florence while Machiavelli was growing up and had died in 1494 but, rather, to his grandson).

   A. When Machiavelli finished *The Prince* in 1513, he dedicated it to Giuliano de'Medici, Duke of Nemours, but the dedication was changed after the duke died in 1516.

   B. He refers to *The Prince* as a little gift.

   C. Machiavelli states his dedication to and knowledge of classical antiquity.

   D. He stresses the value of his political experience.

   E. He points out how he has suffered unjustly at the hands of Fortune.

II. The first chapters of *The Prince* are often glossed over.

    A. They appear to be a catalogue of types of governments or, at least, of principalities.

    B. They do not appear to contain what most people regard as the essence of Machiavelli's thought.

    C. These early chapters are vitally important, however, because they provide a typology of principalities that Machiavelli discusses in *The Prince*.

III. Machiavelli starts with the most basic distinctions.

    A. All governments are either republics or principalities.

    B. This book will treat only principalities, because Machiavelli tells us that he has written elsewhere of republics.

        1. Some see this statement as evidence that Machiavelli began *The Discourses* while he was writing *The Prince*.

        2. Others argue that this statement about his other writing concerning republics was added several years after *The Prince* was written.

    C. He states that all principalities are either hereditary or new.

IV. Hereditary principalities are easy to govern for those who inherit them.

    A. To be a successful ruler is a matter of not breaking old customs.

    B. Princes of unremarkable ability should be able to rule hereditary principalities successfully.

    C. Machiavelli's example is the Duke of Ferrara, who withstood attacks by Venice and the papacy.

V. Before continuing, I would like to pose an important question: How do we make Machiavelli relevant today?

    A. We need to study his works carefully. We cannot pull his words out of context.

    B. Although we may not find an exact parallel to situations that Machiavelli is describing, we can find broader applications in the modern world, for everyone from government office holders to executives and other leaders.

VI. Machiavelli now turns to a prince taking and ruling new territories; because they break with established tradition, such territories are not easily ruled.

  A. It is easy for a conquering prince to find allies, because there are always people eager to change masters.

  B. However, a prince ruling in a new territory always offends those in the territory he conquered and dashes the hopes of those who initially supported him.

  C. A prince needs the support of the inhabitants, who are much less fickle and demanding than noble allies.

VII. It matters whether a new territory is similar in language and customs to that of a conquering prince.

  A. If customs and language are similar, it is sufficient for a new prince to eliminate the old ruling family.

  B. If customs and language are different, one good thing for a new prince to do is to live there.

   1. This is what the Ottoman Turks did in the Balkans.

   2. People want access to their new ruler.

   3. A prince can spot trouble if he is in his new territory.

  C. The best way to secure a new territory of different customs and language is to send colonies there.

   1. This move is inexpensive.

   2. Only those who are dispossessed are injured, and they are, by definition, weak and scattered.

  D. A prince who is in unfamiliar territory needs to make alliances with *less powerful* neighbors.

VIII. The Romans provide a good model for a conquering prince, especially when they entered Greece.

  A. The Romans were able to diagnose problems when they were easy to cure.

  B. Those who wait for problems to become obvious before finding them are often not able to fix the problems.

IX. The negative example is the king of France, Louis XII, in Machiavelli's own day.

  A. Louis committed five specific errors when he invaded Italy.

B. Most serious among the errors was the fact that Louis reduced the power of Venice, although it was Venice that had invited the French into Italy.

X. Machiavelli does history "backwards" in his discussion of why Alexander the Great's empire did not rebel from Alexander's successors following his death.

   A. To explain this phenomenon, Machiavelli looks at two modern political situations.

      1. Principalities ruled by a prince and nobles with an independent power base are easy to conquer but hard to retain. The modern example of this situation is France.

      2. Principalities ruled by a prince and his ministers are hard to conquer but easy to keep once they are defeated. The modern example of this situation is the Ottoman Empire.

   B. The Persian Empire, which Alexander conquered, was like that of the Ottomans and, hence, was hard for Alexander to capture but easy for his followers to retain.

Recommended Readings:

Machiavelli, *The Prince*, translated by Peter Bondanella, chapters 1–5.

Questions to Consider:

1. What is Machiavelli's purpose in presenting a taxonomy of principalities?

2. How does Machiavelli so easily blend ancient and modern examples of an issue he is considering?

3. Why does Machiavelli zoom in on new principalities and how to rule them?

Lecture Six—Transcript
The Prince, 1–5—Republics Old and New

I suppose that all old books have some controversies about them, some things we just aren't quite sure about. One of the reasons for that is because almost never do we actually have the manuscript as it was written by the author. So, you know, you want to read what Thomas Aquinas wrote, the problem is that essentially we don't have any of Thomas Aquinas's, what we would call, autographed manuscripts. Or, we don't have Dante's autographed manuscript of *The Divine Comedy*. Well, we also don't have it for Machiavelli's *The Prince*.

One of the interesting things is, since the book was only published in the 1530s although it was written in 1513, we think there are a couple places where Machiavelli fixed it up a little bit in later years. One of those is the dedication because we're pretty sure that in 1513, when Machiavelli wrote *The Prince*, he wrote it and dedicated it to a guy named Giuliano de' Medici who had the rather interesting title, French title, of the duke of Nemours. But in 1516, he died and, as far as we can tell, Machiavelli changed the dedication, then, to another Medici prince, or as one modern historian has referred to him rather disparagingly, to a princelet. Therefore, as you pick up a printed version of Machiavelli's *The Prince* today, you will see it dedicated—this is confusing—to Lorenzo de Medici the Magnificent. Now, as I mentioned in the last lecture, this is not the Lorenzo *the* Magnificent; this is *a* Lorenzo the Magnificent. In fact, he's a grandson of the one we usually call The Magnificent. The very fact that Machiavelli refers to him as "The Magnificent" like his grandpa was, suggests again that perhaps there's a tone of flattery in the dedicatory letter.

By the way, let me just point out that as I read some passages in our analysis of *The Prince* in the next few lectures, I'll be reading from a new translation by Peter Bondanella. There are many good translations of *The Prince* and it's easy to find references because *The Prince* is divided into relatively short chapters. The book is less than 100 printed pages and there are 26 chapters in it. So, always, I will refer to chapter numbers rather than page numbers, that way whatever translation anybody has it will be easy for him or her to find the passage that I'm talking about. But, I'm using this brand new Bondanella translation—brand new as of, I think, the fall of 2005.

Well, what does Machiavelli say in this dedicatory letter? He says, "I want to send you a gift." And then, almost in a comical way—and Machiavelli's not a laugh-a-minute guy, let's remember—he says, "You know, most people would send you a horse, some nice googah." That's my term, not Machiavelli's. He continues, "but I'll tell you what I'm going to send you. I'm going to send you what I've learned. I'm going to send you a writing that's based on my study of the ancient past, my political experience, my observation of what makes political leaders great. So, don't expect a horse, don't expect some other gift, here is my gift to you." Machiavelli also, at the end, says, "You know, I'm sort of an unlucky guy. I have not been treated very well by fortune." There's a little bit of self-pity at the end of the dedicatory letter, but it is an interesting preface—only about a page long is this dedicatory letter—but it's an interesting preface and it does provide one way of contextualizing what this is about. It is important to remember that it was written as a treatise to be sent to a member of the Medici family and the Medici family was ruling both the papacy and Florence at that time. That is always a good thing to remember, as we turn to the text of *The Prince* itself.

Although it's a short book, it's interesting that sometimes people skim over the first few chapters. It doesn't seem to have a real zing at the beginning. All the famous one-liners are much later on. You know today, when we teach writing to students, we always say you want to start off with something that really grabs you. And, at least from most of our perspectives, Machiavelli does not do that. But, I do want to spend some time on these early chapters because I think they're important both in terms of understanding the book generally and also looking at the M.O., as they used to stay in old detective shows, the method of operation that Machiavelli carries out throughout *The Prince*.

It looks like at the beginning he's going to give us a catalog of kinds of governments. He starts off by saying, "There are a couple kinds of governments. There are, after all, governments that are more or less popular regimes"—what we would call republics—"and there are principalities. There are governments that are in fact run by princes and we need to appreciate the fact that there are both kinds; however," he then goes on to say, "I'm really not going to talk about republics. Because," he says, "I've talked about republics at great length somewhere else." Now, it leads to an interesting question, where does he do that? Of course, the answer is he does it in the other work we're going to spend a lot of time discussing and that is *The Discourses on the First Ten Books of Livy.* "Aha," we perk up and say, "What that means is he's writing these two books simultaneously." If he says, "I've written about republics somewhere else," he must be, at least during the time he's writing *The Prince,* one day working on one and one day working on the other. It's possible. We aren't sure because remember, again, we don't have his manuscript and this wasn't published until about 20 years after it was written and, therefore, it may simply be that a few years later he went back and inserted that. We do know that he began *The Discourses* not long after he wrote *The Prince* and, perhaps, while he was writing *The Prince.* But, we can't take this statement as absolute proof that they were, in fact, simultaneous works.

Okay, so there are republics and principalities; we're not going to talk about republics. Now, principalities, let's make our catalog, our typology, of the types of principalities there are. First of all, of course, there are hereditary principalities—a king dies, a new king takes over. There are new principalities and, therefore, we need to begin to dissect. We don't just talk about all principalities because what might work for one kind might not work for another kind. This is a subtlety that we very often miss when we read snippets of Machiavelli's *The Prince.* It simply seems to be a book about princes and how princes should operate if they're going to be successful and powerful and retain control over their principality. Machiavelli says, "Hey, there are principalities and then there are principalities."

Although he does talk about all kinds of principalities, most of what he talks about in *The Prince* is about new principalities, and there's a reason for that. Hereditary principalities are relatively easy, Machiavelli says. After all, to rule because if you inherit a principality presumably from dad, or occasionally from a brother or an uncle or whatever, first and foremost, you're going to be successful if you just don't mess things up. What you don't want to do is break old customs. You don't want to come in and say, "Well, now that I'm king, I'm going to change the way England or Milan, or whatever it is, has always been." You don't do that. That isn't smart. So, it doesn't take great genius or great skills to continue ruling in a hereditary principality. You have custom and tradition and some unchallenged sense of legitimacy on your side so, in many ways, your job is to not screw things up, to not mess things up. Therefore, he says, there are a lot of successful but unremarkable hereditary rulers, whether it's a king of this or a prince of that or a duke of so and so—those folks, if they aren't bad, they're probably going to make it okay.

Machiavelli gives a contemporary example. He cites, it seems to us perhaps, a fairly minor figure. He cites the Duke of Ferrara. Ferrara's in the northern part of Italy—he was a member of the Este family that had ruled in Ferrara a long time. Let me stop and say the world's never as simple as scholars try to make it and I've talked about the five major states of Italy—Venice, Milan, Florence, the Papacy, and Naples, the Kingdom of Naples, Kingdom of Sicily—but there are several small, still independent, although not big-time players in Italy. Ferrara would be one, Luca would be one, and Siena always was a kind of nemesis to Florence, although more of an irritant than a real enemy at this time. Those are all still little independent states. So, politics is a little bit more complicated than the five I mentioned, but the Duke of Ferrara, he said, "For example, you know Ferrara's a fairly small state. Venice attacked Ferrara, the Papacy attacked Ferrara, but Ferrara survived because, in a sense, the duke was fortunate; he was the heir of a long tradition of Este rulers and he didn't screw things up. He didn't do bad things. He didn't do dumb things. And so, that's sort of enough."

Well, having said that, Machiavelli, of course, now turns to non-hereditary states. He turns to states that are newly conquered; these are the tricky ones because, by definition, they break with established tradition. If you go in and conquer someplace, then, by definition you're changing the rules of the game. However, that place had been governed before; you aren't just the logical successor or the unchallengeable legitimate successor, you're the new guy in town. And so, how do you operate? How, in a sense, do you start ruling from scratch? Now, let me make a broad point here before I go on to talk about this because this is much of what Machiavelli is interested in, in *The Prince*. I said in the very first lecture that we're interested in Machiavelli not just as a figure of the Renaissance, not just even for his historical influence in generations after his, but we're going to constantly ask the question, does Machiavelli have anything to say to us today about politics, as a guide, as a warning, or whatever? How do we make Machiavelli relevant?

First of all, we study the text very carefully. You can't do it by pulling a few words out of context and saying, "Well, as Machiavelli says..." Too many newspaper editorials do this, too many political figures do this, and too many book writers do that. We need to do our homework if we're going to try to do that. But, we have to be creative in saying there is no exact parallel today to a particular situation Machiavelli is talking about. Let's see, though, whether there's some principle here that we can apply in a somewhat, not always perfectly, but a somewhat analogous situation. Let's see if we can find that. So, I ask you, as I'm talking about this text, to think creatively, to think in terms of how do I apply this to a somewhat different world? And, you may find it applying in elements in the United States, in Europe, in Latin America, and in the Middle East. You might say, "Gee whiz, that sort of gives me an insight, an angle, into looking at some particular problem today that I hadn't quite thought of." Machiavelli's not going to give you the answer; he knows that. He's the one who says, in fact, you always have to adjust to every situation because every situation's different. But, there are some principles we can try to extract from Machiavelli that might be widely, although creatively, applicable in different situations. From time to time, I hope to point out examples that are important as I think about politics.

I might also argue that we don't necessarily only have to apply Machiavelli to government. For example, there's a chapter in a recent book on Machiavelli that's called "Machiavelli for the Executive." Therefore, there are other kinds of organizations, not just simply governments, which also have some parallel principles they operate by—parallel to government, that is to say. And so, Machiavelli may not be merely an advisor to government officeholders, but may also be, in a larger sense, a guidebook for certain kinds of leadership in certain situations.

Okay, let's go back to the problem—new states. Somebody has conquered a state or somebody has received a state without it being hereditary or whatever; what do you do? First of all, you find allies; you probably aren't going to succeed and survive on your own. You want to find allies—that is to say, in the territory you conquer. I'm not talking about foreign allies now. You don't just go in and say, "Hi, I'm the king of the forest." You go and say, "Okay, you and you and you, let's work." It's not hard to do because, as Machiavelli points out, there are always people in any state who think they're going to be better off under a new regime. So, you make some allies and that helps you gain power. By the way, Machiavelli points out that he may not necessarily last very long because you can't do everything they want. In other words, let's say I'm sort of a disgruntled noble in a state and here comes this new guy marching in. Why might I ally with him? I might say, "Gosh, he might make me his Chief Minister. Gosh, he might double my property. Gosh, he might let me alone and give me essential independence and jurisdiction over the area that I've traditionally had control of." That might happen. That would be great. That would be good for me. The guy who used to be prince didn't do that; I'm going to back this guy because he will do that. And then, of course, you find out he's got his own ideas or he can't make everybody who's his ally Prime Minister or give him the best job or give him more land or whatever it might be. So, you need allies, but you also know they're probably not going to be permanent because you cannot satisfy their sometimes unrealistic expectations. And, you cannot accede to all their demands, so it's important to understand what you need and the fact that you're going to lose those very allies that help you get control.

And so, Machiavelli makes a very important point here and that is, therefore, what you need to do is develop the support of the inhabitants. The people, the normal, average—you know, Giovanni and Matilda—the peasants or the sort of normal, average folks. You need the support of the inhabitants because they're much less fickle and they're much less demanding than those allies that you needed in order to take over in the first place. It's a very important point that Machiavelli makes because, again, this book's called *The Prince* and it's about princes and it's about tough guys and it's about tough rule. But notice, also, that Machiavelli says the most secure kind of rule you can have is if you have the people on your side and that's an important principle we sometimes forget about.

Now, Machiavelli says, let's make another distinction. Let's say you've conquered a new territory; it matters whether you speak the same language, whether you come from, basically we would say today, the same culture as that territory you're conquering, or whether you speak a foreign language to them or whether you come from a different culture. It matters which one of those is; one is easier than the other. It is relatively easy if the language and culture and customs are the same because you're pretty far along the way once you eliminate the old ruling family. But, if it's a different culture, if it's a different language, you have to have a new set of principles to operate with. Here's what, ideally, you should do. Go live in your new principality and he tells why. First of all, he gives an interesting modern example. He said that's exactly what the Ottomans did when they conquered the Byzantine Empire and the Balkans. The Ottomans didn't just conquer; the Ottoman ruler came to live there and that made a big difference. And so, if you can, go live there. Secondly, this is important because the people want to see their new ruler. They want to have a sense that they have access to their new ruler because, probably, they had some access, however courtly it might have been, to their old ruler. They want to see you around. They want you to be a reality and not an abstraction. Third, he says, you need to be on the scene because troubles will arise and you need to spot them. You need to see what the difficulties are. You need to experience them so you can detect them and deal with them as soon as possible.

Now, he says, often it's not possible for a ruler to go and live in a new territory because, of course, that person might also rule an old territory. So, then, what do you do? The answer is you send colonies. You move groups of people from one place to the other. You have some of your folks living in this new territory. Now, first of all, it's inexpensive. You're not talking about loading up all the vans of stuff; you're talking about moving normal, average people who don't have very many possessions and settling them in the new territory. Secondly, you don't annoy anybody really powerful because, yes, there's some displacement. If these folks are going to get little farms, somebody who has a little farm is going to lose his little farm. But, the people who are dispossessed by the colonies are few in number and, by definition, they're weak and scattered and, therefore, they're not very dangerous. So, it is a very good idea that if you can't go there in person—and that's often the case—you send colonists. You have some of your folks move in among those folks and that's a very good activity.

Now, he says, that's not enough. You also need to make allies with neighbors of the new territory, but you make allies with neighbors of the territory who are less powerful than you. You don't just say, "Ah, there's the obvious ally, I'll sign up with that guy, we'll work out a deal." Because, if that ally is as powerful or more powerful than you, that will not work in your interest because the other society is not signing up to be your ally for your benefit, but for their benefit. And so, what's important is to get less powerful nearby nations, countries, counties, or whatever it might be given the situation, to be your allies. That way they can't get so powerful that they can actually challenge your authority there. Now, Machiavelli gives a good example from the ancient world of how this worked. You may recall from your knowledge of ancient history that in the 2nd century B.C., the Roman republic basically took over the area that today we would call Greece, and the Greek city-states were incorporated into a province of the Roman republic. How did the Romans do that? Well, the point, more than any other one, that I emphasize here is Machiavelli uses an interesting medical analogy. Because the Romans were on the scene, they didn't need to send colonies. What it means is that they were able to see problems when they were tiny problems.

Now, Machiavelli says tiny problems are hard to diagnose, but easy to cure. On the other hand, when a problem becomes obvious, it's easy to diagnose, but hard to cure. That's a very smart medical analogy. We all know that. We hear all the time about, get this test or that test because early detection is the key. Machiavelli knows that; he knows it medically and he believes it works politically. When you've got folks on the scene, when you really are paying attention, you say, "Here is something that could become an ugly problem, we'll deal with it now." But, it takes cleverness, it takes intelligence, it takes focus, it takes a way to get knowledge if you're going to diagnose problems early. Because, again, when they're just starting, they are hard to diagnose. I think that's a very important principle.

Now, Machiavelli takes up this question; he looks at the invasion of the French into Italy beginning in 1494 and says, "Let me study the French because they're a good example of how not to conquer a new territory." And, Machiavelli actually ticks off a list of things the King of France did wrong in Italy. It's very interesting because, in some sense, think about what Machiavelli is doing here; he wants the barbarians out of Italy. He hates the idea of the French coming in. He's writing this book to a Medici; the Medici lost their power in Florence when the French came in and humiliated Florence and they drove Piero de' Medici out into exile. So, what Machiavelli says is, "You know, I don't want the French here. I don't like them, but this is political analysis. The French did five things wrong; let me analyze them." And, one of the things you might say is, "Gosh, I wonder if the French king will ever read this because, essentially, I'm giving the French king a formula for how to succeed in attacking Italy, in invading Italy." It's very interesting that, really, he is giving a lesson to the French king. He even tells a story about the fact that he was talking to a French Cardinal and the French Cardinal was sort of saying that the Italians are not good at a bunch of things.

Machiavelli responds, "And the French are not good at state craft." There's a little zing there.

So, Machiavelli sort of looks at what the French did that was wrong. One of the things he says that they did is the Venetians—that is to say, Venice—sort of urged the French to come in because they were in a struggle with Milan and what the French did was reduce Venice in power, even though Venice had invited them in. That wasn't very smart, Machiavelli says. And so, Machiavelli also helps to look at this French setup and say, let me give you some lessons that we can learn. I'm not going to tick them all off; that's what you do when you read the book, but you can see that, in many ways, what we're seeing in these early chapters is Machiavelli the systematic thinker. There is this catalog of kinds of states and then, sort of dividing the catalog into subparts, then saying this is the way you do things and this is the way you don't do things. Here's an illustration of how you do things, the Romans moved into Greece; here's an illustration of how you don't do that, the French invaded Italy.

I want to end this lecture with a fairly careful look at one particular passage in these early chapters of Machiavelli, where Machiavelli takes a look at an ancient event. Alexander the Great sort of swoops in and, well, I mean this is an exaggeration—we all know that—but he sort of conquers the world. One of the questions that we have to ask is, when Alexander died he was only 33 years old—why didn't that fall apart? Why didn't the areas that he conquered, the Persian Empire, whatever it is, why didn't those folks all rebel against his successors? How were Alexander's successors able to hold on to this territory? Machiavelli says, "Let me tell you how I'm going to go about answering that question. I'm going to take a look at two nations today that are very different, and I'm going to analyze them and I'm going to suggest that one would be easy to conquer and hard to hold, while the other would be hard to conquer and easy to hold. And, I want to use these contemporary illustrations of what the differences are between a place that's easy to conquer and hard to hold or hard to conquer and easy to hold. And then, when I learn that lesson from these nations that I'm looking at, if you will, up close and personal, where I've got lots of information because these are contemporary, these are nations that are functioning right now, then I think I'm going to have a better historical insight into why Alexander the Great's successors were able to hold on to his empire."

Very often, we think about the fact that what we do is analyze the past and study history, and that gives us an insight into the present. Machiavelli is saying that it works the other way, too. Let's take a look at the present, let's take a look at the way things are functioning, and see what lessons we can draw from those contemporary situations and, then, that might help us to answer some very difficult questions about the past. There's a kind of dialogue, if you will; the lessons go both ways between the past and the present. It's a very interesting point that Machiavelli makes. What nations are we going to talk about? We're going to talk about the nations of France and the Ottoman Empire. What he says is that France is a principality—it's a kingdom, but he's used the term principality, generally ruled by a prince and his nobles. In France, there were a lot of dukes and counts and all this sort of stuff. Now, he said, a place like that is actually pretty easy to conquer because you've always got nobles who are discontented. You can always find some allies inside who say, "Gosh, I'll back this guy because nasty old king so-and-so is taxing us too much," whatever it is. But, he says, "Those kingdoms are hard to hold because you can't satisfy all those guys and those nobles think they're as good as you are." That's what nobles are; they're hereditary, they've got the blood, and they say, "What does this guy know about this kingdom? Why, we all have some theory that says we are the equals of the king." So—France is easy to conquer, hard to hold.

On the other hand, there is Ottoman Empire, which is ruled by a ruler and his ministers, people he appoints. There's no traditional nobility. It's hard to conquer because all the guys that have power work directly for and their fortune is related to the power of that ruler. To conquer it, you've really got to clobber it, but once you conquer it, it's easy to hold because of the fact that you don't have a hereditary class that says we're as good as them, we're as good as the new rulers. The Ottoman Empire is the example of that. Therefore, he says, when you look back at Alexander the Great and his conquest of the Persians, what do you discover? Persia was like the Ottoman Empire. Alexander the Great, it took a hell of a lot of work to conquer it and beat it, but once you beat it, it was beaten, it was conquered, and it was yours. That is one of the most interesting early lessons we learn from *The Prince*.

Lecture Seven
The Prince, 6–7—Virtù and Fortuna

Scope:

We first look at two terms that Machiavelli uses often, *virtù* ("virtue") and *Fortuna* ("fortune") and what they mean when he uses them. We then approach chapter 6, which concerns new principalities conquered through the prince's own skill. In it, Machiavelli will cite such diverse figures as Moses; Romulus, the legendary founder of Rome; Theseus, the legendary Athenian; and even Girolamo Savonarola, the Dominican friar who dominated Florentine politics immediately following the expulsion of the Medici in 1494.

Chapter 7, which deals with territories acquired by fortune or by the arms of others, is one of the most famous in *The Prince*. Here, Machiavelli introduces his readers to Cesare Borgia, often referred to as Machiavelli's hero or role model for a modern prince. Machiavelli, while an ambassador for the Florentine Republic, had met Borgia, and certainly he admired many of Borgia's "Machiavellian" traits.

Outline

I. Let us define a couple of words that Machiavelli uses often, *virtù* and *Fortuna*—words whose English equivalents do not always do them justice.

   A. The Italian word *virtù* is hard to translate and requires some explanation.

   1. The word comes from the word for "man" in Latin. Hence, it came to mean "manliness."

   2. Machiavelli believes that *virtù* is also the way to practice statecraft successfully. That is, one needs to be somewhat aggressive, even cruel—*manly*, exhibiting and practicing *virtù*—in order to maintain power in most situations and keep the state stable.

   3. Machiavelli uses the word in a variety of ways, sometimes with more traditional meaning and sometimes with this newer sense.

B. Machiavelli recognizes that the concept of *Fortuna* is quite different in classical and medieval texts and tries to reestablish the classical notion.

    1. In the classical world, Fortune was said to be a woman and could, to some extent, be controlled or its effects influenced.

    2. In the Christianization of the concept of Fortune in the Middle Ages, it came to be associated with fate and was considered totally out of human control. Dante used the image of the wheel of fortune over which we have no control, implying that Fortune spins the wheel and determines the good and bad with regard to material possessions.

    3. Machiavelli returns to a more classical definition of Fortune, feeling that some things are out of our control but maintaining that we can be prepared for Fortune and her effects.

II. In chapter 6, Machiavelli exhorts his readers to study history in order to see what *virtù* is, especially the deeds of great men, and to see how people have dealt with *Fortuna*.

    A. Machiavelli lists several great conquerors, including Moses, Theseus, and Romulus, and argues that Fortune gave them only the opportunity to create new principalities; it did not make them succeed.

    B. One of the most difficult tasks these new princes had was to establish new political institutions.

        1. Those who prospered under the old institutions would always oppose those who create new ones.

        2. Those who did not prosper under the old institutions would still be lukewarm about the new.

III. Machiavelli draws one of his most important conclusions when discussing princes who succeed because of their own virtue.

    A. The new prince must be able to use force.

    B. Armed prophets succeed while unarmed prophets fail.

        1. The most recent example of an unarmed prophet was Girolamo Savonarola in Florence.

        2. A good ancient example of an armed prophet who succeeded was Hiero of Syracuse (3rd century B.C.).

IV. In chapter 7, Machiavelli presents and analyzes the story of Cesare Borgia (also known as Duke Valentine), son of Pope Alexander VI.

    A. Alexander VI sought a territory for his son to rule within the lands controlled by the Church.

        1. Alexander obtained French troops for Cesare's use.

        2. Cesare became a new prince, successful in conquering the Romagna, but he found himself in a difficult situation because he had relied on troops not his own.

    B. Cesare Borgia eventually lost what he gained and died a defeated man, despite the fact that he did just about everything right.

    C. Cesare won the Romagna by Fortune, then used treachery and deception (*virtù*) to establish control.

    D. Cesare realized, however, that the French troops were not sufficient for him to maintain power, and he recognized that he needed to build his own army.

    E. He won favor with the Romagnols by establishing order and security.

        1. He employed a cruel man, Ramiro d'Orco, and gave him full authority to establish law and order in the Romagna.

        2. Ramiro did what he was told to do but inevitably was seen by many as cruel and ruthless.

        3. Cesare had him executed and his body displayed publicly to show the Romagnols that the cruelty of Ramiro was not Cesare's doing.

    F. Cesare had plans to expand his rule into Tuscany and other parts of Italy.

    G. In order to carry out his plans, Cesare worked hard to control the College of Cardinals and, hence, the papal election when his father died.

        1. Cesare did not have enough cardinals under his control to choose the next pope, but he had enough to veto anyone unacceptable to him.

        2. His father, Pope Alexander VI, died unexpectedly while Cesare himself was ill.

        3. Cesare allowed the election of the mean-spirited Julius II. This move was Cesare's only mistake.

        4. As a result, Cesare lost all that he had conquered.

H. Despite all of Cesare's skill and brilliance, the one mistake he made was fatal.

I. Still, Machiavelli believed that Cesare should be imitated in his ability to reduce dependence on others' troops and establish his rule in the Romagna.

Recommended Readings:

Machiavelli, *The Prince*, translated by Peter Bondanella, chapters 6–7.

Questions to Consider:

1. What does Machiavelli mean by the word *virtue* (*virtù*), and how do we deal with this concept given that the word really has no English equivalent?

2. In what ways does Cesare Borgia manifest *virtù*? What was the role *Fortuna* played in Cesare Borgia's life?

3. Can we argue that Cesare Borgia displayed *virtù* in his sometimes violent governance of the Romagna?

Lecture Seven—Transcript
The Prince, 6–7—*Virtù* and *Fortuna*

I want to begin this lecture by trying to define, or at least attack from a number of angles, a couple of words and concepts that Machiavelli uses where the modern English equivalent, as you'll find in any translation, just doesn't fully tell us what Machiavelli has in mind. One of those terms is the Italian word *virtù*, which is almost always translated as virtue; the other is the Italian word *Fortuna*, which we translate, of course, as fortune. Machiavelli uses both of these terms a great deal. What I want to argue is that he's really giving us something of a new definition of *virtù* and, with regard to fortune, he is sort of passing over what happened to that concept in the Middle Ages and going back to a more classical definition of it. Therefore, it's worth pausing because in all of Machiavelli's works, he uses both of these words a great deal.

When we say somebody practices virtue, what we tend to mean is they're kind and gentle and sweet and loving and prudent and temperate, and all the other things. But *virtù*, we need to appreciate, comes from the word for man—that is to say, *vir* or *were* in classical Latin—and therefore, it is a word that implies a certain manliness. But more than that, what Machiavelli wants to argue is that *virtù* is the way you practice statecraft successfully. It's nice if in practicing statecraft successfully, in practicing *virtù*, if you are nice and gentle and kind and loving, and there may be situations where that is sufficient and fine. Machiavelli is not against those things. But, what Machiavelli argues is that one needs to be somewhat aggressive and manly in order to maintain power in most situations and that sometimes means cheating, lying, deceiving, and carrying out acts of cruelty. Those can be defined by Machiavelli as *virtù* because, after all, those are things that keep states stable. I think Machiavelli would probably, in some ways, agree with what King Creon says in Sophocles's play *Antigone*. That is that chaos, anarchy, is the worst of all things. Nobody has any rights. No human relations can exist when there is chaos and, therefore, to bring about and keep order is, indeed, to practice virtue, as Machiavelli understands the word.

Now, like many authors, he doesn't always use the word *virtù* to mean exactly the same thing. Sometimes when he uses the word, it seems to mean something traditional, something like a dictionary definition that we would have today. But many other times, he uses it in this new sense and it's important when reading *The Prince* to have this in mind because, usually, from the context, one can determine whether he's using this word in a traditional way or whether he's applying a somewhat new definition. So, be aware that every time you hear me say the word virtue, or if you read *The Prince* in English and you see the word virtue, or if you read it in Italian and you see the word *virtù*, keep in mind that one needs to ponder a little bit exactly how Machiavelli is using that word.

The second term is fortune, or *Fortuna* in Italian. In ancient times, it was said that fortune is like a woman and, therefore, to some extent—this is not me now, this is classical authors, keep in mind—in some way, then, fortune can be controlled and its effects can be influenced. We can do things to affect fortune. However, as Christianity came into the world as a dominant religion in the West, the term fortune came to change. For example, Dante has the image, and he doesn't create it, but he's the most famous use of it perhaps, of the "wheel of fortune." What Dante says is that fortune spins the wheel, and the wheel determines with regard to material possessions and we really have no control over the wheel, which is constantly spinning. In other words, fortune has come to mean something like fate, something we endure, but something over which we have no control. Machiavelli is going to go back to a more classical definition of fortune and, therefore, there are certain things that happen over which he have no control. He will use the very famous image at the end of the book, "Fortune is like a river." We'll talk about it more then, but basically, fortune—well, there are floods. We can't stop the rains from coming, we can't stop the snow from melting in the Apennines and filling the rivers, but we can be prepared for fortune. We can build levies and dikes and dams and whatever. And so, there's interplay between things outside our control and things that we can modify the effects of; those are both parts of the idea of fortune. Fortune does not mean fate for Machiavelli. And so, I'm going to be using both of those words beginning with some of the analysis in this lecture and throughout our discussions of Machiavelli, and I simply want to be aware of the issues of these two very important words.

Now, let me suggest that Machiavelli says directly to his readers, "You know what to do? What you need to do is study history. You need to see what *virtù* consists of, how successful rulers have operated. You need to see how people have dealt with fortune."

Again, it doesn't matter, in a sense, if everything is fated, because then you don't make any choices. But if you believe in his definition of fortune, then what you need to do is see how people have prepared for it and responded to certain acts over which they had no control—everything from natural disasters to an unexpected death to whatever it might be. And, if *virtù* has to do with keeping control and keeping power and keeping order, then obviously what it consists of at any particular situation is going to be different from another situation because of the uniqueness of circumstances. So, if we believe in his definition of fortune, if we believe in his definition of virtue, we need to do a lot of serious study, he says.

Let me take a look at some of the great conquerors of all time and, by the way, they include a much broader list than you would expect. Of course, he would mention a Roman like Romulus or a Greek like Theseus, these semi-legendary figures that come out of classical antiquity, but among the great conquerors, he also includes Moses. He's read his Exodus as well as his Livy and his Greek history. And, he says that fortune gave them the opportunity to create new principalities. Fortune gave them the opportunity. Fortune didn't make it succeed. Fortune didn't determine the outcome. What fortune does for these guys—and they are guys, of course—is to give them certain opportunities and it's important to take a look at those opportunities.

Now, once you've been given the opportunity to conquer a new territory, the question is, what do you do? How do you establish new political institutions? Okay, you've been given the opportunity. You've taken advantage of the opportunity, and now what do you do? Well let's start with this; there are always people who prospered under the old rule who will oppose any new rule. If you're very close to the top in a society and somebody new comes into rule, you'll recognize that you're probably going to descend in terms of power or whatever it might be. Secondly, even those who didn't particularly prosper under the old realm are going to be suspicious of the new realm. It isn't to them clear or necessary that they will be lifted up or the people above them will be brought low. The point, of course, that Machiavelli makes is that this is hard. It's a lot easier to fail than succeed, even if fortune, some particular thing over which you had no control or very little control, gives you an opportunity. That isn't enough. You can't say, "Gosh, God opened the Red Sea for me to lead these people and form a new society." That isn't enough.

Without some sort of opportunity, you can't do it, but opportunity doesn't equal success. And so, Machiavelli says if you've been in a sense blessed by a fortune, you then need to practice virtue. You need to go out and be successful by your own virtue. You must be willing and able to use force. This is not always nice. You've got to be willing to use force. You've got to be willing to be tough.

One of the most famous phrases out of the many famous phrases in *The Prince* is Machiavelli saying that, "Armed prophets succeed"—Moses would be a good example—"while unarmed prophets fail." Here's somebody who has an opportunity and a vision of a new society. You need to do that and be armed. His great example of an unarmed prophet is Girolamo Savonarola; we talked about him in the previous lectures. This is, after all, the Dominican preacher who was a very important leader in Florence and he was a mesmerizing speaker. He would preach in the cathedral. He would organize, especially, young men to sort of carry out moral reform, but ultimately, he depended only on his own ability to persuade and inspire. There was nothing there to support his movement and, of course sooner or later, it went wrong. And, which we now, within four years of Savonarola really taking the leadership in the founding of the new republic following the expulsion of Piero de Medici in 1494, Savonarola was executed in the main square in Florence. In fact, one of the newest and finest biographies of Savonarola has the title *The Unarmed Prophet*. It's become a phrase that stuck to Savonarola. Again, I want to point out that Machiavelli had a great deal of respect for Savonarola. He was brilliant in what he did, but it wasn't enough. He was not able, ultimately, to bring his vision, his idea of this new society to bear because he didn't have the wherewithal to do it. Being a great speaker isn't enough.

There's a difference, he says, between an armed and unarmed prophet. By prophet here, there's no religious connotation; prophet means somebody, in a sense, with a vision of a new society, a new structure. Machiavelli contrasts that with a figure who's a fairly minor figure for us today, unless you're really a classical historian, a guy named Hiero of Syracuse. He tells the story of Hiero of Syracuse in southern Italy, in Sicily. He tells the story of Hiero and how Hiero had a vision to take over and how he executed that vision armed with military support. He tells that Hiero, whatever you think of his vision, Hiero was successful. Ultimately, Savonarola wasn't. So, it's an interesting contrast that Machiavelli gives between—and he does this so often—an ancient example and a modern example.

Chapter 7—there are 26 chapters in *The Prince*—chapter 7 is, to me, a particularly important one because here Machiavelli pauses, it seems, to tell stories of a man whom he knew personally and a man who he deeply respected, but a man who ultimately failed. This is Cesare Borgia. Cesare Borgia was the son of Pope Alexander VI, a member of the Borgia family. And, if you recall I mentioned this briefly earlier in a previous lecture, one of the main goals of the pontificate of Alexander VI was to provide a territory for his son to rule forever, ideally, and a husband for his daughter Lucrezia Borgia. Well, of course, there's been a lot more ink spilled over Lucrezia Borgia than there has been over Cesare, but Machiavelli spilled his ink over Cesare Borgia.

He says let me take a look at this guy because he conquered an area of Italy, he was a new prince; he was not hereditary. He conquered an area that's called the Romagna. Now today, if you look a map of Italy and you see it divided into the 20 political regions of Italy like Tuscany and Lombardi and whatever, one of those regions is called Emilia-Romagna. The capital of Emilia-Romagna is Bologna; it was north of Florence. This is the more eastern part of Emilia-Romagna, much of it very hilly, very difficult territory to hold, and not a territory dominated by major cities. We sometimes think of Italy as very, very urban; the Romagna is not a particularly urban part of Italy. And so, Cesare Borgia goes to carve out this territory for himself. Now he has, if you will, fortune. For one thing, Daddy is pope and Daddy can get him some troops. And, Daddy does get him some troops; he gets him some French troops. And so, Cesare is able to take over the Romagna not actually grabbing it by any great *virtù* of his own, but largely because there was opportunity. Dad was pope; French troops were available to help him.

And so the question is, what do you do with it? I've got the Romagna, now what? Well, let me fast-forward to the end. Cesare dies a defeated man. And yet, many people talk about people Cesare Borgia as the hero of Machiavelli. Let me just point out, parenthetically, because if you read things about Machiavelli you need to know that Cesare Borgia's name is that, but he also has a title—he's sometimes referred to as Duke Valentine or Valentino, but they're all the same guy, Cesare Borgia. I'm going to call him

Cesare Borgia—that is, after all, his given name. So, it seems odd that Machiavelli's hero is a guy who ended up defeated. But, Machiavelli looks at him, looks at his career, knew him personally, and said this guy did almost everything right. He made one big mistake at the end that cost him everything and Machiavelli doesn't try to cover that up. Cesare Borgia, if he is Machiavelli's hero, is a flawed hero, and a big flawed hero. But, what Machiavelli sees is that Cesare got the Romagna by essentially good fortune and, then, by the practice of *virtù*, he took control. He set up new institutions and he brought order to the Romagna, no mean feat as it turns out.

Perhaps more than anything else, Machiavelli looks at Cesare Borgia and says, he realized that those French troops were not sufficient. Because when you use somebody else's troops as he did to conquer the Romagna, you're in the debt of and, in some ways, under the control of the person supplying the troops who, after all, can always un-supply them. And so, he says, Cesare Borgia recognized that what he needed to do is build his own army, an army of his own troops who were loyal to him, not lent to him as the French troops were. This is unusual in Machiavelli's day because most of the wars that were fought in Italy in Machiavelli's day were fought with mercenary troops—sometimes foreign, sometimes Italian—but mercenary troops. The papacy had Swiss troops. You still see the Swiss guards in the Vatican and so on. And, as I pointed out in my biographical lecture of Machiavelli, Machiavelli as an official of the Florentine republic tried to make Florence less dependent on mercenaries and build some sort of force from the men in the Florentine city-state, primarily in the countryside. And so, Machiavelli sees as part of the *virtù* of Cesare Borgia that he did not rest on the fact that lent troops conquered the Romagna for him. Again, that's the opportunity, that's the *Fortuna* part. It's *virtù* that will keep that territory.

Now, one of the problems with the Romagna was that it was a mess. In particular, it was disordered. It's a hard place to police. Again, it's hilly and it hadn't had strong government for awhile. And so, there was theft and brigandage and all the rest that you associate with a place that doesn't really have an effective government. How does Cesare Borgia make the Romagna his? You bring, if I may use a phrase, law and order. People want security. People want to be safe. Farmers want to take their goods from their farm to the market. People want to travel for commerce, or for that matter, on religious pilgrimage. And, they don't want to be mugged when they get outside the walls of their city. And so, Cesare Borgia recognized the essential quality of bringing order. How does he do it? He used, as his employee, if you will, a Spaniard whom we know as Ramiro d'Orco. And, Ramiro d'Orco was tough. He imposed law and order, we would say today, without a lot of niceties. We would say today, he did it without being very attentive to people's civil rights or due process—now, these are terms I'm introducing from a later time, but this is a guy who played tough. You find somebody who's a thief, you don't spend a long time with the trial, and you lop the head off. This is tough stuff.

We know that creating order out of chaos is tough business and Ramiro was one tough guy. And, you always offend certain people when you act that way, even if the result is the place is getting a little bit more peaceable. There are always people who say, "I don't want to see body parts scattered around that Ramiro has chopped off of a thief," or whatever. And, "After, all that thief is somebody's son," or "He's somebody's father." You always offend people and, again, Ramiro d'Orco was tough. Machiavelli said that Cesare knew that when he appointed him and, clearly, Cesare knew what he was doing and thought that was okay because the goal is order and security and stability, which also, of course, will strengthen Cesare as the ruler of the Romagna. And then, Cesare made what is regarded by Machiavelli as one of the brilliant moves. One day in the city of Cesana, which is in Romagna, people awoke and came to the main square and there was Ramiro d'Orco, half of him in this part of the square and half of him in that part of the square. He had been sawed in half and he had been laid out in two pieces. Now, we would say, that's pretty cruel, after all this guy was hired to do a job, he did it, and clearly he did it with the consent of the person who hired him, Cesare Borgia. But think of what this did. First of all, it says, hmm, Cesare's a pretty tough guy himself, he's in charge. But more than that, it said Ramiro sort of went over the line and Cesare didn't let him get by with that and, therefore, in a sense, we come to like Cesare more. This is because when he saw one of his own officials being sort of too mean and too tough, he said, by cutting him in half, "I'm not going to put up with that."

Now, again, we can look at Cesare as one of the great hypocrites of all time. He knows what this guy's doing, he approves of it, and now that he sees it's in his interest to do so, he saws him in half as a way of saying, "I'm on your side, I'm a good guy. I have limits to what I will tolerate in terms of reaching the goal of order and stability." He gets the best of both worlds here, Cesare does. Machiavelli sees this as brilliant because, on the one hand, Cesare has gotten some law and order in the Romagna and he's gained in popularity and respect with the citizenry for sawing this guy into two pieces. By the way, notice he didn't kidnap him, he didn't hang him out in the woods; he saws him in half and props him up in the main square. I mean we just have to picture this visually. You come into town to buy your melon to go with today's prosciutto in the market, and there's this guy on both halves of the piazza—pretty dramatic, pretty public. Word spreads fast; you don't need newspapers when you do something that dramatic, word spreads very fast. Everybody knew what it meant. Everybody knew who was responsible for slicing Ramiro d'Orco in half; it was Cesare Borgia. And so, Cesare Borgia becomes not the hero to Machiavelli, I don't think that's the right word, but he does become a model of *virtù*; somebody who has achieved something through fortune and now says, "I'm going to make it work and I've got to figure out how to do it in the particular situation of the lawlessness of the Romagna." And, Cesare had plans to expand his territory beyond the Romagna into Tuscany, which is, after all, where Florence is.

But Cesare didn't do that. One of the other plans of Cesare was that when Daddy died, he could name, ideally, the next pope. Meaning that he had enough cardinals in his pocket that he could choose the next pope. Well, he never got to that point, but he did have enough cardinals in his pocket that he could veto any candidate for pope. So, he didn't have the control he hoped to get over the College of Cardinals, but he had enough to have a veto power because it takes two-thirds of the cardinals to elect a pope, then as now. Well, what happened was Alexander died—that is to say Alexander VI, Cesare's father—died unexpectedly. He died at a time when Cesare was very ill and this was a bad combination. In fact, a pope was elected who only lived for about a month, Pius III, and then they come back to another conclave. We all remember that happening in 1978 when John Paul I died after about a 30-day pontificate.

Cesare Borgia allowed Pope Julius II to be elected; this, Machiavelli said, was his mistake. Julius was a military man, mean-spirited—go watch the movie *The Agony and the Ecstasy*. He's the guy that commissioned Michelangelo to paint the ceilings of the Sistine

Chapel, where he's always yelling at Michelangelo; he really wasn't a very nice man. Mean, war-like, military, he led troops in battle himself. Cesare could have gotten those cardinals who were in his pocket to veto the election of Julius, but he didn't and that was his undoing and, as a result, he made one fatal mistake and that did in everything Cesare had so brilliantly, through the practice of his *virtù* after the opportunity given him by fortune, had carried out. And so, Cesare's an interesting lesson and, again, Machiavelli saw this up close and personal; he was actually with Cesare Borgia on a diplomatic mission for Florence at the time Alexander VI died. So, Machiavelli saw all of this upfront, up close. Despite the fact that it all ended in tragedy with Julius II becoming pope and really sort of putting an end to the rule of Cesare over the Romagna, Machiavelli still looks at Cesare as the model of *virtù*—not a flawless model, but a model. The way he tried to get control of the College of Cardinals, the way he brought in his own troops, and the way he used cruelty well—a term Machiavelli will use, "cruelty well"—in his manipulation of and the death of Ramiro d'Orco. And so, in this dramatic portrait of this man Cesare Borgia and only a very few pages in chapter 7, we have one of the most dramatic sets of lessons that Machiavelli teaches us in a book full of lessons.

Lecture Eight
The Prince, 8–12—The Prince and Power

Scope:

Machiavelli's ninth chapter of *The Prince* examines civil principalities, leading to a discussion of the prince's relationship with the citizens he governs. Some might be surprised by Machiavelli's claim that it is more important for a prince to have the people than to have the nobility on his side.

In chapter 11, Machiavelli takes up the particularly Italian issue of ecclesiastical principalities. After all, the popes claimed direct temporal rule over a large part of central Italy. In this context, Machiavelli makes some interesting remarks about the relationship of the Church to contemporary politics.

Machiavelli creates a brief catalogue of the types of soldiers that princes make use of and makes the claim that there can be no good laws without good armies. Hence, it is essential to have the right kind of army.

Outline

I. Machiavelli next takes up the matter of princes who acquire their territories through wickedness.

   A. He provides one ancient example, Agathocles of Syracuse, and a recent example, Oliverotto of Fermo.

   B. Both of these men achieved power by wholesale killing of important people.

   1. Machiavelli believed that one may acquire power but not glory by killing one's fellow citizens.

   2. He points out that cruelty can be well or badly used.

   a. It is well used if it is done all at once and out of necessity.

   b. Cruelties that increase over time are doomed to failure.

   C. Although Machiavelli qualifies his comments about cruelty, he recognizes that an evil, such as slaughter of fellow citizens, can indeed be well used.

II. In chapter 9, Machiavelli discusses civil principalities, that is, those obtained through the consent of citizens.

    A. This can be done in one of two ways:

        1. Through the people.

        2. Through the nobility.

    B. It is more difficult to retain a principality obtained through the nobility, for they believe themselves to be the prince's equal.

    C. Common people are more easily satisfied than nobles, and thus, it is easier to retain a principality that they have given to the prince.

    D. Nobles want to oppress others, while the people simply do not want to be oppressed.

    E. Princes need the support of the people simply because there are so many of them.

    F. There is no fixed way of winning the people, because circumstances are different in each situation.

III. Machiavelli asks what the proper way of measuring a prince's power is.

    A. The question is whether a prince can stand on his own or needs the protection of others.

    B. In particular, a prince must fortify his city.

        1. The best examples of such fortified cities in Machiavelli's day are the independent cities of Germany.

        2. They have walls, moats, and artillery.

        3. They have provisions for a year, including the raw materials that will allow citizens to continue their employment.

        4. It is almost impossible for these cities to be besieged successfully.

IV. In chapter 11, a discussion of ecclesiastical principalities, specifically the papacy, completes Machiavelli's "catalogue" of princely states.

    A. These are the easiest principalities to maintain because they are rooted in ancient religious institutions.

B. Before the French invasion of Italy in 1494, there was a balance of power among the five major powers of Italy (Florence, Milan, Venice, Naples/Sicily, the papacy), brought about by the Peace of Lodi in 1454. This balance of power kept the papacy weak.

C. When this balance of power was destroyed, Popes Alexander VI (and his son Cesare Borgia) and Julius II were able to increase significantly the power of the papacy.

D. At the time that Machiavelli writes *The Prince*, Pope Leo X (Giovanni de'Medici, son of Lorenzo the Magnificent) rules in Rome, and Machiavelli is hopeful that the papacy will reach new heights as a result of the pontiff's goodness and virtue.

V. Machiavelli then turns to a prolonged discussion of the types of troops that princes employ.

    A. He observed that states need good laws and that where there are good armies, there are good laws.

    B. There are three kinds of armies:
        1. A prince's own troops.
        2. Mercenaries.
        3. Auxiliaries or troops borrowed from other states, as with the French troops that Pope Alexander VI provided to his son, Cesare Borgia.

VI. First, Machiavelli discusses mercenaries, stating that they are worthless.

    A. In wartime, the enemies plunder a prince's territory, and in peacetime, his mercenaries plunder his territory.

    B. Good mercenary captains are untrustworthy, and bad captains have no value.

    C. Carthage in ancient times and Milan in modern times have been taken over by their mercenaries.

    D. Florence has been fortunate that its mercenaries have not done more damage to that city.

    E. Venice is a good case study because it was successful militarily only as long as it used its own citizens in war.

    F. Machiavelli concludes that mercenary captains have led Italy into servitude.

Recommended Readings:

Machiavelli, *The Prince*, translated by Peter Bondanella, chapters 8–12.

Questions to Consider:

1. What does it mean to say that cruelty can be well used, pondering Hamlet's famous comment that sometimes one has to be cruel to be kind?

2. What can we deduce about Machiavelli's views of commoners and nobility?

3. Is Machiavelli right when he insists that only a prince's own troops have any value to him?

Lecture Eight—Transcript
The Prince, 8–12—The Prince and Power

We've seen so far, although I've stopped along the way to talk about a lot of detail with regard to certain pieces, that Machiavelli's being very systematic in the way he lays out kinds of government. There are republics and there are principalities; not going to talk about republics. There are hereditary principalities; not going to talk much about them and there are new principalities. Okay, now we've done another subdivision. There are new principalities that are conquered through fortune, that we looked at last time. Now, we turn to, there are new principalities that are conquered through wickedness.

The example that Machiavelli gives is, again, one of those that his audience would know better than we do, unless we're really geared up to classical history—a guy named Agathocles of Syracuse. Perhaps, also to dramatize this, and perhaps recognizing that we might not know Agathocles real well, Machiavelli also gives a modern example from one of these minor states in Italy, a guy named Oliverotto of Fermo. Again, I'm not going to go into detail about these guys; you can read a little bit of their background in *The Prince* and also in translations like the one I am using. There are fairly detailed, sort of mini-biographies even of the minor characters of *The Prince* that are very useful. But here is the question—how do you understand, how do you deal with, how do you explain, how do you analyze, do you praise or do you blame those who conquered territories, through wickedness? Machiavelli says, "Well, it's possible to attain power by just killing lots of folks." That's one way to do it and that's what these guys did. "However," Machiavelli says, "You acquire power, but not glory when you kill a number of citizens."

Now, one of the questions we might ask Machiavelli is how important is glory as opposed to power? In other words, how do we deal with the fact that some of these guys who come and kill a lot of people end up being successful? Again, they have an idea of a society they want to create and they come in with knives flying and they are able to take over and create that. Machiavelli deals with this in one of the most famous passages in *The Prince* and I actually want to read this to you and then we can talk about it a little bit. "Many others," he says:

> …employing cruel means were unable to hold on to their state even in peaceful times, not to speak of the uncertain

times of war. I believe this depends on whether cruelty be badly or well used. Those cruelties are well used, if it is permitted to speak well of evil, that are carried out in a single stroke, done out of necessity to protect oneself and then are not continued, but are instead converted into the greatest possible benefits for the subjects. Those cruelties are badly used that, although few at the outset, increase with the passing of time, instead of disappearing. Those who follow the first method can remedy their standing both with God and with men as Agathocles did. The others cannot possibly maintain their position.

This is a language that's very disturbing to a lot of people: "cruelty well used." We want to put cruelty and well used in separate categories and make them exclusive of one and another, but Machiavelli says cruelty can be well or ill used. Again, the very language shocks us and Machiavelli knows it shocks us. This is nonsense to Aristotle. This is nonsense to Cicero. These two great venerated classical authors, these two great thinkers whose political ideas have so penetrated the culture of Western Europe, even more so during the Renaissance, and now Machiavelli talks about well-used cruelty. It reminds us that this is a different book and a different kind of book, in some ways, that's ever been written in the West. Again, even though it follows the form of other mirrors of princes, we need to appreciate how staggeringly different this is. And you can imagine today, as well as in Machiavelli's own day, how people respond to phrases like that—"well-used cruelty." You just did something cruel, well done in this case, or badly done—either way.

Today, we find things such as a book entitled *Machiavelli's Virtue*, which argues for a kind of need to understand Machiavelli as a political thinker who has described realities that we need to take very seriously. We have Leo Strauss, the famous 20th-century political thinker, referring to Machiavelli as a "teacher of evil." It's one of the great Machiavelli questions, a new political morality, political amorality, political immorality being justified. What is it? I don't want to give you an answer. I want to give you, of course, the notion of what Machiavelli says so that you can think about this and explore this and relate it to other things and you give the answer. That's what's important—not a determined end in the course, but the opportunity to empower everybody to think a little bit differently, to wonder whether the categories, the boxes that we create, are the only possible boxes or are the best boxes in which to put things. And so, I think when we hear a phrase like "well-used cruelty," it reminds us that Machiavelli is, to use a phrase that we use perhaps too much in the 21st century, thinking outside the box, or we might say, a new paradigm of political thought and political behavior.

But notice what Machiavelli says—Agathocles, he's an example of somebody who used cruelty well, did it early, did it all at once, and got on with things. And, he says both people and God will forgive that kind of cruelty. Again, we have to ask, "What did it lead to? What did it permit or make more likely to happen?" That Syracuse, where Agathocles is, is a more stable, a more ordered, a more secure place and if that is so, isn't that cruelty well used, Machiavelli asks? Or, do we simply say cruelty is always unjust, it leads to bad consequences—that's certainly what Cicero would say—and therefore, once we hear cruelty, we already know where to classify this guy, bad guy, tyrant, whatever label we want to put on it. And so, Machiavelli really is challenging. He was challenging in his own time. He was challenging, of course, to the ideas of Cicero and Aristotle, also challenging traditional Christian morality. He was challenging what's being passed down as the word of God through interpretations of scripture, through ways that people read what Jesus said, and tried to find the political implications. Jesus didn't talk very openly and directly about politics, but Jesus certainly gave moral lessons that many people believe are meant to apply in the macrocosm, as well as the microcosm of the individual person.

Machiavelli is challenging all that. One of the ways he's challenging it is, he says, if what you're trying to achieve is a certain vision of a society and you aren't there yet, the question is how do you get there? What's legit to get there? These are, I think at least we ought to take this away from it, these are perhaps tougher questions than we might have thought. We need to look from a variety of perspectives. We may decide Machiavelli, as Leo Strauss did— there's nobody smarter than Leo Strauss in a lot of ways—is just simply a teacher of evil. Or, we might decide something very differently, but a passage like the one I read you, I think, is one that does indeed stimulate us to think and ask whether our boxes, our labels, and our paradigms are the only ones there can be.

Next, Machiavelli turns to what he calls civil principalities. These are principalities obtained through the consent of citizens, not through some violent intervention, but for example, sometimes when a city-state is in trouble, it will bring in a prince to rule. It happened very briefly in Florence. The Florentines figured out they made a mistake and kicked him out; that was back in the 14th century when the Duke of Athens was brought in. Milan and other cities did that and those folks stayed and even sometimes established dynasties. So, the question is let's look at principalities that begin with people bringing in somebody from the outside. Now, first of all, Machiavelli says—again, notice how he's sort of doing this wonderful structure of political possibilities—it can be done in two ways; one is you can be brought in by the people by a kind of popular movement or you can be brought in by the nobility. He says it is more difficult to succeed if you're brought in by the nobility because—and I've mentioned this before about nobility—nobility think you're their equal and they're your equal and, therefore, they might bring you in, but they don't like being dominated by you. They don't like being dominated by you. They don't like following your rules. They sort of bring you in thinking of themselves as equals and thinking of themselves as trying to have as much autonomy as possible.

Then, of course, we can draw the conclusion that it is easier to succeed if you were brought in by common people. And here, Machiavelli makes a very interesting distinction; he says that nobles—hereditary nobility, people with titles, people sometimes who have legal privileges in society—nobles want to oppress other people, but the people only want not to be oppressed. It's a very interesting distinction. If you're trying to satisfy nobility, you are trying to satisfy people who want to oppress others who want to maintain their legal, or economic, or political advantages. And, it's hard to do; if you're trying to order a state, it's hard to do that. But, people want not to be oppressed. People sort of want to be left alone. They want to be allowed to live their lives with as little intervention by the government, whether that's taxation or that's rules they have to play by or military service they're obligated to have, or whatever, and so the people are easier to keep happy. Furthermore, he says, there's another advantage of the people that we don't want to forget and that is there are simply so many of them. Nobles are a very small group and nobles, even a few of them, can turn against you with your destruction coming next. But, a few people turning against you—and you can't please all people all the time, as we know—a few people turning against you will not ultimately lead to your downfall. And so, their very number makes them a safer group to support you.

Then, Machiavelli makes another important point and that is how do you win over the people? His answer is a tough one for us. There is no formula. There is no fixed way. What you have to do is look at the circumstances. History can provide examples and from those examples we might be able to derive principles, but one of the principles is you've got to be flexible and go with the situation. It may be possible in some societies to satisfy people with, what we called in Roman times, bread and circuses. In other times, it might be that those particular ways of keeping the people happy won't work. And so, any ruler who wants to be successful in winning over the people needs to figure out what the people want so that they can be won over. And again, I think what Machiavelli is saying is you can't look it up in a book. You need to study history, you really need to study history hard and seriously; he emphasizes this over and over again. Remember the work we're going to look at next is a systematic study of early Roman history as recorded by Livy. Studying the past is an awfully good guide, but one of the things you do is not find one-to-one correspondences. "Ah, here's some guy back in the past and what he did was try to win over the people and he did X and, look at that, he won over the people, therefore I'll do X." That is the wrong lesson. Maybe X will work, but X won't work in your situation because it worked in his. You've got to be really sure there is a parallel situation. It may take something radically different than what X did to succeed in your situation.

And so, sometimes when people think about the study of history or people who, as Machiavelli does, constantly bombard us with historical examples, that what we're supposed to do is draw up this treasure trove of things to look up. This is the way I always think about it; the one thing I really wanted more than anything in the world was a Junior Woodchuck's Guidebook. For those of you who were Huey, Louie, and Dewey fans, as I was, whatever situation—I mean, the Duck boys would be in the weirdest, oddest situations and somebody would say, "Pull out your Junior Woodchuck's Guidebook and look it up." And there would be an answer of how to deal with that particular problem. I always thought, "God, I want that book. It must be a very thick book. I want that book." What Machiavelli says is there no Junior Woodchuck's Guidebook. There is no treasure of trove of examples where you simply say, "Ah, I'm going to look up one that is sort of like the situation I'm in, and I'm going to do exactly what they did back then because I can assume the result will be the same."

It doesn't work that way. But, one always needs to be very alert to the present and the past. That's the best guide. Notice that all through Machiavelli's *The Prince*, that's exactly what he does. He gives us examples from the distant past—after all, we live a lot closer to Machiavelli's time than Machiavelli did to ancient Greece or Rome. He goes way back and looks at the past and then, he also gives us a number of examples from the present. Again, going back to the first one I used in this lecture, people who got their territories through wickedness— Agathocles 1,800 years ago and Oliverotto of Fermo a few years ago. We need to be aware of both and recognize changes and differences.

Now, the next question Machiavelli asks is how do we measure a prince's power? How do we know who's doing well? How do we know who is successful in ruling? Any of you who've read resumes know that all resumes look good. Here's a particularly important answer for Machiavelli. A prince who is successful is a prince who can stand on his own, rather than needing the protection of others. That's a pretty interesting definition. Can stand on his own, meaning he has an army, has people administering the various branches of the government, the justice system, whatever it might be that a prince who does not rely on others needs to keep in power. Again, that was the great secret of Cesare Borgia. Other troops, the troops of the French put of Cesare Borgia into power, then what does Cesare do? He gets rid of them and organizes his own troops. There is a prince who really does have power because men loyal to him are the ones who are in the field and so on.

Now, Machiavelli is interested not just in government, but he's also interested in, to some extent—we'll see this more in *The Discourses*— what we might call the technology of war. It's very interesting because here, his examples of well-governed civil principalities come not from Italy and not from the ancient world; they come from Germany. Remember Machiavelli traveled to Germany. I've already mentioned something he did when he was in France dealing with the French monarchy; here's something he learned while he was in Germany. He says the best examples of what I'm talking about are various independent cities of Germany. Remember, Germany's not a country at this time any more than Italy is a country at this time. Germany is a big mish mash of church-ordered states and princes and kind of independent cities and all sorts of different arrangements. But, he went to some of these independent cities of Germany.

Here's what they've got; they've got walls, they've got moats, and they've got artillery. Of course, not too long after this, artillery won't be as useful; Machiavelli doesn't know that. He said, but more than that, they have provisions for a year, including all the raw materials that citizens will need to continue their employment. Not just food, you've got to have more than food inside your city walls or more than water, although you need those things. You need also not to have, if your city is under siege, everybody unemployed. People need to have the raw materials to make what they make whether it's purses or cloth or something made out of iron or whatever it is. And, he said when you see a city that's been organized that way you know that that city really can function on its own, it's not dependent on anybody else because if it's ready for a year—sieges don't last more than a year, normally—there is a place that really is secure and independent. There is a place where whoever rules that city really has something, really has power, and really has things under control.

Again, I want you to notice how broad Machiavelli's look is; he looks at the Italy around him that he knows very well. He looks at classical antiquity, which he knows very well. He looks at France because he was there. He looks at Germany and things he learned there. This is a man, you sort of get the picture, that every night, no matter what he was doing, he'd go back and take some notes, "What I've learned today." He seems to have had, in a sense, a kind of one-track mind. "I'm really interested in politics and how governments work and how power is achieved and how power is maintained and how power is extended." And, he's always looking for something that will enlighten him, always looking for an example, always looking to build up that treasure trove of information—not so he can duplicate it, but so he can enunciate principles. Again, Aristotle did that, collected all this information, but the difference is Aristotle's goal was to figure out how states ought to be ideally; Machiavelli's was how things work. It was how things work, what really works and what really doesn't, and so this is a very interesting notion.

Now, Machiavelli finally gets to the end of his catalog and he talks about ecclesiastical principalities and, although that might be a little city-state in Germany that was run by a local bishop—there were a lot of those—primarily, of course, he's thinking of the papacy. He says, these are the most fortunate of institutions; their rulers are really the ones who are best off because they're easy to maintain because they're rooted in religious institutions and claim the authority—obviously we're talking about a Christian world now—of scripture. It's one thing to rebel against a bad prince; it's another thing to rebel against God's representative, if you take God seriously. After all, the papacy was an office that was seen as a successor of Peter and the vicar of Christ, and even if the guy is sort of a bum, he's still the successor of Peter and the vicar of Christ and you're going to challenge that very, very seriously. You're going to think about it before you say, "I'm going to take on God's representative on earth."

Machiavelli points out that, therefore, the papacy has certain advantages over other kinds of principalities, even hereditary ones. I mean this is even better than hereditary principality in a lot of ways and how, therefore, was the papacy kept in check in Italy? The answer is in 1454, Cosimo de Medici and others worked out this deal—I refer to it in my narrative of history—called the Peace of Lodi, or Lodi. In this deal a kind of balance of power was achieved between the five main players in Italy—Venice, Milan, Florence, the Papacy, and the kingdom in the south. Now, what happened? The French invaded in 1494, remember I've told you the French change everything? The French invaded in 1494 and that messed up this balance of power; that said all bets are off. It lasted 50 years; well, 40 years, who cares about a decade now and then? Just kidding. It lasted from 1454 to 1494 and then, the French invasion messed all of that up and it allowed the papacy to start saber rattling again; it allowed papal expansion. Alexander VI, the father of Cesare Borgia and Julius II, for all practical purposes, his successors were both men who were intent in expanding the Papal States. That was bad for Italy. So, ecclesiastical states had an advantage. In the second half of the 15th century, that advantage was mitigated by the wisdom of people like Cosimo de Medici and the kind of peace that was set up in Italy. But when that was broken, it allowed again for aggressive popes because of their intrinsic advantages to become aggressive again and that further messed up Italy. So, the French just don't mess up Italy because they're in Italy, they also mess up Italy because they ruin that balance of power and they allow the papacy, once again, to do things that are damaging to Italy in general.

Having said that, let's not forget that at the time Machiavelli wrote this book, the pope is Leo X, a member of the Medici family, and therefore, Machiavelli notes that he thinks that the papacy will become a more positive institution in Italy. He thinks that it will work toward making things better, better than it has under the two predecessors of making things worse with Leo X there because of Leo's goodness. So, there is perhaps a touch of optimism, perhaps a touch of flattery in what Machiavelli says, in what essentially is the end of this catalog of the kinds of governments. Republics—we're not going to discuss them. Principalities—okay we have what kinds of principalities? We have those that are hereditary—not going to discuss them much; those won by fortune, those won by ugliness and violence, those won by people being invited in, and those that are ecclesiastical. Our catalog now is essentially complete and we turn to some other issues.

Issue number one that Machiavelli turns to once this catalog is finished is what makes the best armies? Because he says that states need good laws and where there are good armies, there are good laws. This goes back again to the difference between an armed and unarmed prophet; that if you're going to have good laws and good laws that are effective—and by the way, army here doesn't just mean fighting a foreign foe because we need to remember armies did, what we would call, a lot of the police work of the time. There were no police forces; there were no, in modern Italy *carbineri* or whatever. Army means men at arms and, of course, men at arms might patrol your own roads for burglars, as well as be part of an army attacking a foreign nation or defending itself against a foreign nation. So, you need good arms because you really are not going to have good laws without them. And, if you have good laws and no arms, that's not going to work either.

So, what kind of an army can you have? Once again, Machiavelli is being systematic. There are three kinds of armies: you can have your own army, you can have an army that's bought for you—that is to say, mercenaries—or you can have an army that's sort of lent to you, which he calls auxiliaries. You can have your own army, a mercenary army, or an auxiliary army. An example of the third, by the way, would be the French troops that were sort of lent to Cesare Borgia through the machinations of his father in order for Cesare to conquer the Romagna. Now, he says, lets start by discussing mercenaries. They are worthless. They are worthless. In wartime, he says, the enemy plunders your territory because, very often, these mercenaries really aren't the best fighters. After all, they're fighting on contract. They're not fighting for something they love, they're not fighting for patria, for country; they're fighting for a paycheck. And so in wartime, your enemies plunder your territory, and in peacetime, your own soldiers plunder your territory because they are foreigners by definition and when they're unemployed or if the paycheck is late, they get rowdy. And by the way, there are many, many examples in Italian history to indeed justify what Machiavelli has to say.

He says good captains of the mercenary forces are untrustworthy and bad ones are even worse. There is no such thing as a good mercenary army; there is no such thing as a good mercenary commander. They're all on the take. They go to the highest bidder. They aren't as courageous in the defense of your country because it isn't their country. And so, Machiavelli gives some examples, again ancient and modern; Carthage and Milan in modern times were taken over by their mercenaries. Florence, he said, has actually been lucky. Florence has depended on mercenaries for centuries and they've only been mildly disastrous. They haven't been totally disastrous as they have been in other places, for example, Venice. Venice, he said, won battles as long as they had their own trips; when they joined the sort of Italian system of mercenaries, that's when they began to lose. And so, mercenaries are the worst kind of army. They have, in fact, more than any other single factor, perhaps led Italy into servitude. How could the French march in and be so successful so quickly? How could that encourage other foreign troops to come in? The answer— well, here are the first three answers—mercenaries, mercenaries, and yes, you got it, mercenaries.

Lecture Nine
The Prince, 13–16—The Art of Being a Prince

Scope:

Chapter 13 contains Machiavelli's denunciation of the common practice of his day for Italian city-states to rely on auxiliary soldiers. In his discussion in the following chapter of how a prince prepares himself for war, Machiavelli stresses practical exercises of both mind and body and the necessity of studying history.

Machiavelli also lays out part of what is new in his political thought by pointing out that human weakness lessens the value of those in the past who have written of ideal, imaginary republics. Such works will not get a prince very far, for often he must act in less-than-ideal ways in order to be an effective ruler. Machiavelli also contrasts having a particular virtuous quality, such as generosity, and appearing to have it. Which is more vital for a ruler?

Outline

I. In chapter 13, Machiavelli argues that auxiliary troops are also worthless.

    A. If they lose, a prince is destroyed; if they win, the prince becomes their prisoner.

    B. Machiavelli prefers modern to ancient examples, citing the fact that Pope Julius II, Florence, and the Byzantine Empire put themselves in the hands of auxiliary troops.

    C. While mercenaries are dangerous because of their cowardice, auxiliaries are most dangerous when they fight well.

    D. Cesare Borgia (Duke Valentine) conquered the Romagna with auxiliaries, then used mercenaries but saw their danger and eliminated them, finally turning to his own men.

    E. The first sign of the Roman Empire's destruction was when the Romans hired the Goths to guard the frontier.

II. In chapter 14, Machiavelli writes that war is the principal art of a prince, and it must ever be on his mind.

    A. A prince stays in shape for war through exercise and study.

        1. Hunting is a good activity for princes.

2. A prince should get to know his land well and think constantly about how he would deal with a military situation in the mountains, hills, valleys, bodies of water, and so forth.

3. The most important subject of study is history.

   a. A prince should study successful princes of the past and understand why they succeeded.

   b. Many great princes have imitated those who went before them; for example, Julius Caesar imitated Alexander the Great.

B. It is vital that princes prepare for war during times of peace and tranquility.

III. Machiavelli begins chapter 15 with a reflection on writers of the past who have imagined perfect states, no doubt referring to Plato and Cicero, among others.

A. People so lack in perfection that anyone following one of those writers about imaginary states will certainly fail.

B. A prince must learn how and when not to be good.

C. It is acceptable for a prince to have a reputation for those vices without which he could not preserve his state.

D. Apparent virtues often lead to ruin, while apparent vices lead to success.

IV. Machiavelli considers the differences between being generous and being perceived as being generous.

A. Those who win a reputation for generosity will usually fail because of what they have done to gain that reputation.

   1. Sumptuous behavior will win a reputation for generosity but will be too costly.

   2. Such behavior will ultimately require more revenue, hence higher taxes, leading to the prince being hated by the people.

B. It is those who are seen to be miserly who have accomplished great deeds.

   1. Pope Julius II and the kings of France and Spain are reputed to be miserly, but they have been successful.

   2. A reputation for being miserly actually makes it easier for a prince to rule successfully.

V. When a prince spends his money and that of his people, he should be tightfisted, but he should be generous when spending the money of others.

Recommended Readings:

Machiavelli, *The Prince*, translated by Peter Bondanella, chapters 13–16.

Questions to Consider:

1. How can a prince study war in times of peace, and why is it necessary to do so?

2. Do theoretical works of politics, for example, Plato's *Republic*, have any value for those who rule?

3. Is being a successful prince all about creating illusions and covering up reality (perhaps today we would say "spinning")?

Lecture Nine—Transcript
The Prince, 13–16—The Art of Being a Prince

In the previous lecture, we transitioned from a catalog of the various kinds of governments and kinds of princes there are, into a look at the prince, and especially the prince and the way he fights for or defends his state. Machiavelli is very much interested in war; he wrote a book called *The Art of War*. His biography of Castruccio Castracani is a biography of a great warrior of the 14th century. He is very much interested in the military side of things. And, if you recall where we left off last time, Machiavelli said there are three kinds of armies you can have. You can have your own army made up of your own citizens and that's good. You can have mercenary troops, a bought army—a rented army, if you will—and they're always bad. There's a third kind of troops, auxiliary troops. Auxiliary troops basically are those you borrow. As we saw last time, the good example of that is that Cesare Borgia won the Romagna largely with French troops that his dad the pope had arranged for him to be lent from the French king. And so, having rejected mercenaries, what we talked about at the end of the last lecture, let's look a little bit at what he has to say about auxiliaries.

He says you lose, no matter what the outcome of the battle, if you have auxiliaries because if they lose a battle, you are destroyed. If they win a battle, then you, the prince, become their prisoner. So, if you win, you lose and if you lose, you lose and so auxiliary troops are of no value. Machiavelli, as he so often does, cites several examples of nations that have not done well because of their reliance on auxiliary troops. Here's one of the places though, it's sort of odd, where all the examples are modern. Certainly, there are illustrations from antiquity, but Machiavelli really focuses in on his own time and he lists three leaders, three political territories that have suffered because of the reliance on auxiliary troops: Pope Julius II, the successor, more or less, of Cesare Borgia's father Alexander VI; the city of Florence, which relied on auxiliaries from time to time; and the Byzantine Empire, which after all had come to an end in 1453.

Machiavelli looks around; why did the Byzantine Empire come to an end? There are lots of answers, but one of the answers is they didn't have their own troops; they relied on auxiliaries. Machiavelli knew this, by the way, from his own study of the history of Florence because there was an ecumenical council held in Florence in the

1430s that Cosimo de Medici sort of organized. It tried to bring about the reunion of the Greek and Latin churches because the Greeks knew they were going to fall to the Turks unless they got some military help from the West, but they weren't going to get any help militarily from the West as long as the eastern and western churches were in chasm. And so, that council, on the surface, was about religion. To a great extent, it was about politics, and even though an agreement was reached in Florence, that agreement was never essentially ratified back home in Constantinople and, therefore, there was not the kind of military presence that was needed in the Byzantine Empire to overwhelm, or at least drive away, the Turks.

Now, Machiavelli also draws an interesting comparison between mercenaries and auxiliaries. He says mercenaries are dangerous because they're cowards. You're out there in the battlefield to get a paycheck and you might say, "Hey, damn it, this is dangerous. I don't want to get myself killed for a paycheck." So cowardice is very common among mercenary troops; however, Machiavelli says, it's when the auxiliary troops fight with courage that you're in trouble. Okay, it's when they really do fight hard and so every kind of army except your own has fatal disadvantages. One of the most interesting passages, I think, is what Machiavelli writes in this context about Cesare Borgia. Remember Cesare Borgia conquered the Romagna with French troops, but then tried to install his own. Let me read you this passage from *The Prince*:

> I shall never hesitate to cite Cesare Borgia and his actions.
> This duke [remember he was also known as Duke Valentine]
> entered the Romagna with auxiliary troops leading an army
> composed entirely of French men and with them he captured
> Imola and Forli. But not considering such troops reliable, he
> turned to mercenary forces, judging them to be less dangerous
> and he hired the Orsini and the Vitelli. When he found, in
> managing them, that they were unreliable, disloyal, and
> dangerous, he got rid of them and turned to his own men.

This is a guy that had all three kinds of armies. Again, Machiavelli knew him up close and personal because he had been part of a Florentine diplomatic mission to Cesare Borgia and, therefore, although, as we saw, Cesare Borgia is someone Machiavelli looks to, we need to remember Cesare Borgia ended up losing everything.

Nevertheless, on this particular point that Machiavelli sees as so crucial and where Machiavelli thinks the Italy of his own day is so wrong-headed, Cesare was right on and he praises Cesare Borgia.

His last comment on these different kinds of soldiers, and in particular on auxiliaries, is interesting because he turns to a period he doesn't discuss very often, the end of the Roman Empire in the West. The end of, what we would call, antiquity in the West. He says, as I look at the collapse of the Roman Empire, what do I attribute it to? I think the first sign of destruction of the Roman Empire, Machiavelli says, is when the Romans hired Germans, Goths, to guard the frontier. Remember, Rome had some natural frontiers like the Atlantic Ocean, for example. The empire also had tough land borders, the Rhine-Danube frontier being the most important. For awhile, especially after some depopulation in the Roman empire, the Romans found themselves bringing Goths across the Rhine, in particular, and sort of semi-Romanizing them and hiring them. What they hired them to do was go fight the rest of the Goths to defend the Roman Empire against their fellow Goths as soldiers in pay of Rome. And so, this is a bad idea. It was a bad idea in antiquity. It's a bad idea now, Machiavelli says. Interestingly, in the 18th century when the fall of the Roman Empire got its classic interpretation from Edward Gibbon, if you say, we'll take that 2,000-plus-page book of Gibbon, what did Gibbon see as the reasons for the decline and fall of the Roman Empire? Number one was barbarians coming from the outside and, of course, the weakness was that the barbarians were being called upon to fight against the other barbarians and, secondly, it was the nature of Christianity taking over the Roman Empire. So in that way, in many ways, Machiavelli anticipates what Gibbon is going to say in the 18th century about what are the major reasons for the collapse of Roman authority in the West.

Machiavelli then continues to talk about the prince as a soldier and a commander of soldiers, but he changes topics. War, he says, is the principle art of a prince and it must ever be on his mind. I guess the way we would say that today is a little bit different; that the number one job of the commander in chief is to provide for the security of the people whom he, or now she, may govern. And so, Machiavelli says let's talk about the prince as a warrior and as a warrior chieftain. How do you prepare yourself for war? How do you train? What do you do to be ready when military action is needed? Well, you do two things; exercise—you need to be strong because, if you will, the prince as commander in chief in those days didn't sit in an office, he was on the battlefield and therefore, you needed exercise. The second thing you needed was study. You needed to read, you needed to observe, and you needed to think. Here's a list of some activities that Machiavelli says are vital for a prince, especially in times of peace. Hunting is a good activity for princes because you get some exercise, you're riding around on a horse; but also, you're getting to know the lay of the land. You're getting a feel for how hard it is for a horse to make a turn or go up a hill or down a hill or cross a stream or whatever it might be, because in hunting you really have a sense of what you and your animal, and therefore this military unit, can and cannot do. That's very important because I think Machiavelli is suggesting, how many people have planned strategies militarily without thinking about the lay of the land, without thinking about what the capabilities are of the various animals that are going to be carrying the soldiers? And so, hunting is a good way to practice. It's a good way to sort of stay in shape, both physically and mentally, he argues.

Secondly, he says, whenever a prince is traveling—and princes move around a lot, we need to remember—they need to constantly look at the land and they need then to imagine: I'm riding along on the road and I say, now look there, look at that hill. Now, if there were enemy soldiers on that hill, what position would I want my troops to be in down here? Or, where might be the place where they are most vulnerable and where's the place in this landscape that I would be most vulnerable if I had my troops? And so, you're constantly exercising your mind. You're not riding along, off to the next town for whatever purpose, listening to your whatever the 16th-century version is of an Ipod. What you want to be doing is thinking, planning, imagining, scheming, strategizing, and conceptualizing because you don't have time to do that on the job training. When you are at war, when you are besieged or when you need to attack, that's not a good time to start thinking "Gee, how do you deal with troops that are stationed on top of a hill?" Or, "how do you get across a particular body of water and how do you look for a place to fork the stream?" That's not a good time to do it when the other guys are out there. Machiavelli new a lot about battles that Florence had been involved in, as well as other city-states in Italy, as well as the history he had read, to know that you need to be prepared. You don't start thinking about war when war breaks out. When you do, if you're not doomed, you're certainly at a disadvantage.

Then Machiavelli says, let's talk in a more formal way about what princes should study, because princes should read. What should they read? First and foremost, they should read history. Now, history certainly means something a little bit different than it means to most of us today. Today, we think about intellectual history and social history and cultural history and economic history; we think about the history of common people where we might read about a labor movement or whatever. That's not what Machiavelli means. He means history in a more political and military sense because most history that was written, including Machiavelli's own history of Florence as we shall see in subsequent lectures, is about leadership and it's about military activities. You read Thucydides's *History of the Peloponnesian War*, for example, and you say, "Gee, what are women doing at this time?" After all, women take on different roles. Women's lives changed during the Peloponnesian War as well as the men who were actually out in the field; you would hardly know that from reading Thucydides. He focuses on the politics of war and the battles that took place in the war. That's sort of the heritage that Machiavelli is inheriting from the classical history he knows, and so you need to read history. You need to see which princes were successful militarily and what the causes of their success were.

You obviously, contrarily, need to look at the princes who failed and figured out what the nature of their failures were. Furthermore, Machiavelli says, we need to remember that some of the greatest military victors in history have consciously seen themselves as following in the footsteps of predecessors that they read about. One of the examples that Machiavelli gives is that Julius Caesar modeled himself on Alexander the Great. And so, it is very important to look to the past and to learn from the past. Now, as we're going to discover in later discussions of Machiavelli, this doesn't just mean go see what Julius Caesar did and do exactly as Julius Caesar has done; it doesn't mean that because, of course, no two situations are exactly the same. Therefore, you may learn a strategic hint, a strategic idea from a great military prince of the past, but that doesn't mean you do exactly what he did way back then because you've got to always take into account what the principal was behind that action, and maybe that principal requires a different specific choice or action today than it did then because the world isn't the same. That you may look with admiration at Alexander the Great or Julius Caesar or any other one of these folks, but if you're in Italy, you're not conquering the Persians. If you're in Rome, you are not necessarily doing what Julius Caesar did. You may have the same landscape, but politically, the situation's different; technologically, the situation is different.

So, although Machiavelli urges the study of history and imitation here, we're going to see how much he reflects on that and how much he refines that notion both in *The Discourses* and also in the *Histories of Florence* that he writes. Even towards the end of *The Prince*, he's going to come back to this issue a little bit. Again, in finishing this section, Machiavelli makes the point that you study for war during times of peace. That is the proper time to prepare, to think, to strategize, to imagine—to study. When those guys come over the hill invading your territory, you don't say "Gee, let me get out my history book and do a little thinking about how I should fight." That's not the time you do that. You do it in times of peace.

Machiavelli then turns to, in one of the most famous passages of *The Prince*, a sort of reflection on the kind of political science that he is creating here and how it differs from the past. I want to read you an extraordinarily important passage; this is at the beginning of chapter 15 of *The Prince*, just a few lines into the chapter, if you're following along in the text. "Many writers," he says, "have imagined republics and principalities that have never been seen nor known to exist in reality. For there is such a distance between how one lives and how one ought to live that anyone who abandons what is done for what ought to be done achieves his downfall rather than his preservation. A man who wishes to profess goodness at all times will come to ruin among so many who are not good; therefore, it is necessary for a prince who wishes to maintain himself to learn how not to be good and to use this knowledge or not to you use it, according to necessity." Let's break that down into the two main components.

First of all, he said in the past a lot of folks have written about places that we'd like to have, places that there ought to be. Now, automatically, it seems to me, what comes to mind to most people who are familiar with the Western tradition is Plato's *Republic*. Although no doubt, here he's also referring at least as much to Cicero as he his to Plato's *Republic*. Now, he doesn't say throw those books away. What he says is, though, they're a different kind of inquiry than I'm making because their goal is to define what ought to be. My goal is to define what is, to see how the world works right here, right now, and then figure out how to act in it effectively. I'm not about the "oughts" of the world; I'm about the "this is the way things are." This is a real shift because, as Machiavelli says, if you follow that line with me, then what we know is that you've got to learn not to be good. In Plato's *Republic*, obviously you need just rulers. Justice is the topic of Plato's *Republic*. If you had to reduce Plato's *Republic* to one word, it would be justice. For Cicero, the prince needs to be loved, the prince needs to be virtuous, needs to live according to honesty and kindness and whatever. Machiavelli says if princes live like that, given the way people are, they're going to lose. They're going to be defeated and— let's not forget that Machiavelli really cares about this—the states that they govern are going to be open to attack and they're going to become chaotic. And so, what a prince needs to learn to do is not be good sometimes. Then, it doesn't mean you go out and start not being good; what it means is if you know how to be good, then you need to know next when not to be good.

You may know what it means not to be good, but you may always be good, because the times may never require not to be good. You'd have to be really lucky, probably, but it is not something you automatically do. You say, ah, I've learned not to be good and now let me go out and show everybody I know how not to be good. You need to use that knowledge carefully and you need to use it with a goal in mind. Machiavelli here is making a very interesting point about what we would call political realism. Now, Machiavelli then raises the question, what happens if in fact you are not good and—well, this is going to happen—people notice it? Machiavelli says, it's all right for a prince to have a reputation for those vices without which he could not preserve his state. If you have to be a little bit cruel, then you'll survive with the reputation of being a little bit cruel. I remember in the 1960s, Margaret Chase Smith, senator from Maine—at that time the only woman in the senate at a time of a great deal of civil unrest in the United States—said on the senate floor that if people are given a choice between chaos and despotism, they'll choose despotism every time. They'll choose a strong leader rather than anarchy. Machiavelli's basically saying here that if a prince is able to preserve his state and keep order by being not good, sometimes it's okay to do that and it's okay even to have the reputation of doing that. People don't look to their princes as moral models; they look to their princes for order and stability and protection, and it's very important for Machiavelli to make that point.

Then he uses—remember, I talked about this earlier—the term virtue in the way I'm going to describe it now, in the traditional way. Remember, there are two ways to talk about virtue; virtue as this sort of manliness, this sort of what you need to do to preserve the state, but also we know that virtue retains its traditional meaning, all the nice things that you are. Machiavelli says apparent virtues often lead to ruin, while apparent vices lead to success. Being not good is an apparent vice, but it can lead to success. Being kind is an apparent virtue, but it can really mess up the world; it can really mess up the state you're in. So, we need to distinguish between what appears to be true virtue and the reality of what is virtue, and Machiavelli's going to come back to this point more times in *The Prince*. We're going to look at a passage later on that's going to focus in on this issue of apparent vices and virtues and real vices and virtues. Machiavelli then turns to another quality of princes and that is generosity. Again, it's a traditional virtue, especially for Cicero, that princes should be generous. Machiavelli says let's hold on; those people, those princes who win a reputation for generosity, will usually fail because of what they have done to gain that reputation. Think about that. In other words, I want to be seen as having the traditional virtue of generosity, so what do I do? Well, what does it mean to be generous? You give a lot of stuff away. You hand out things here and there to various people or to all the people, depending on exactly the kind of state you have. But, Machiavelli says, to do that, to live out according to that apparent virtue, is going to really get you in trouble.

Let's talk about why. Sumptuous behavior, which is one way that some people would define generosity, will win a reputation for generosity, but it'll be too costly. If you give a lot of stuff to everybody—guess what—you run out of stuff. Or, if you don't run out of stuff, you've got to get the stuff that you're then going to give away. What will that mean? Well, the example Machiavelli gives is if you are too generous because you're working hard to develop a reputation for generosity, if you're too generous, you're going to need to raise more revenue. Now, how do you get more revenue? This is easy, we don't need to go back to the 16th century to know this one; you raise taxes. But, remember what Machiavelli said way at the beginning? It's very important for princes to have the people on their side. Now, we all know this one, too. How do you lose the support of the people? Read my lips, is the answer to that question.

That is to say, if I, as the prince, in a way of sustaining the development of my reputation for generosity say that in order to do that I've got to tax you more, I've got to take a bigger percentage of what you make, your income, your property, whatever the basis is for taxation, you'll be surprised how quickly I'm going to lose my reputation for being a good guy, despite the fact I have a reputation for generosity. Generosity isn't going to save me. Here are the choices—would you rather have a prince who is just lavishly generous? Or would you rather have a prince that keeps taxes down? That's the question, the way Machiavelli puts it, and Machiavelli says the people will choose not having higher taxes, not having more of their property confiscated. This is because most people never think they get their confiscated property back. They see it going someplace else.

And so, Machiavelli here is making very careful observations about the fact that the successful princes need the support of the people— remember, people are less fickle than the nobility and, therefore, you need the people. If you try to create a positive image of yourself by being exceptionally generous, you'll ultimately end up taxing more of the very people who you need to be on your side. That's what happens. And so, Machiavelli gives a very interesting and careful observation about the need for being very careful with the wealth that you have to spend as prince. And, Machiavelli gives several examples of successful princes who had reputations for being miserly. They're all contemporary examples. One is Pope Julius II— again, he was pope in the very beginning part of the 16th century. He dies in 1512, if I recall, maybe 1513, so Julius II is a good example of this. The kings of France and Spain in Machiavelli's own day are good examples of people who were miserly, who had a reputation for being miserly, and who were nevertheless successful. In fact, he says, a reputation for being miserly actually helps princes be successful, not the sort of common sense notion that, gee, I need to look generous in order to be successful.

I remember a few years ago I was on a panel for the National Endowment for the Humanities, and we were helping to decide who was going to get certain grants, and I remember taking my position of miserliness. I said, "Here's a grant proposal. Gee, if it were just me, if it was my money, I'd fund this. But this is not my money I'm helping to decide about; this is the people's money and I don't think the citizens ought to be sponsoring this." I might think it's a good long-shot proposition, but I don't think that's something I, as a citizen, should be investing in and so I tried to make that distinction and, essentially, it's a Machiavellian notion that when you're handling somebody else's money—that is to say, the people who pay the taxes—you better be damned careful with it.

Now, Machiavelli then goes on to say, when the prince spends his money and the money of his people, he should be tightfisted. But, if you get somebody else's money, meaning you conquer a territory and win some wealth, you get certain spoils of war, then you should be generous. Be generous in spending other people's money. Be tightfisted spending your own and the money of your citizens. And so, what we see here in this section of *The Prince* is that Machiavelli, after having looked at the number one job of the prince, which is security, which is to take care of the principality, to prepare for war, and to execute a war plan, if and when necessary, we now turn to those other qualities that allow the prince to govern successfully. Because, after all, being simply a military guy, being a tough guy, isn't enough. You need the support of the people. How do you get the support of the people? You need to have a base of power that even if you have a great deal of authority, even if you've taken a territory by force, you've got to govern it, and what won it for you won't keep it for you. And so, we see here, and in the next few chapters we'll be looking at beginning in the next lecture, we're going to see how Machiavelli is molding an image of the prince as someone who not just conquers a territory, but actually orders it, administers it as well as defends it.

Lecture Ten
The Prince, 17–21—The Lion and the Fox

Scope:

Should a prince be loved or feared if indeed he cannot be both? Traditional thinkers would have chosen the former, while Machiavelli argues that the right answer is the latter. Similarly, Machiavelli asks if it is necessary or wise for a prince always to keep his word.

In chapter 19, the longest of *The Prince*, Machiavelli draws on an extraordinary range of historical and modern examples in exploring how princes can avoid being hated. In doing so, he offers subtle lessons about how a prince today should use the past without imitating it literally. The lesson Machiavelli teaches here has applications for anyone who wants to learn from, but not be beholden to, the past.

Outline

I. A prince should be thought merciful, but it is important to be clear about what is cruel and what is merciful.

  A. Cesare Borgia was cruel, but his actions brought order to the Romagna.

  B. Machiavelli contrasts Borgia's actions with the "mercy" that Florence exercised that allowed the neighboring city of Pistoia to be destroyed in bitter and violent internal factional disturbances.

  C. Was not Borgia really merciful and Florence really cruel?

II. Machiavelli asks whether it is better to be feared or to be loved.

  A. Of course, it is best to be both.

  B. However, it is better to be feared than loved.

  1. The reason is rooted in human nature; people are fickle and deceptive.

  2. Men will more likely attack someone loved but not feared than vice versa.

  C. Princes should avoid being hated.

  1. Princes should not take property from those governed.

2. Nor should they do violence to the women of those governed.

D. One of Machiavelli's most evocative examples from antiquity is his discussion of Hannibal's cruelty.
1. Historians praise Hannibal for keeping his army loyal and disciplined in a foreign land for many years.
2. People criticize Hannibal for his inhuman cruelty.
3. They fail to realize that Hannibal kept order in his army precisely *because* of his inhuman cruelty.

III. In chapter 18, Machiavelli argues that a prince must be like both a lion and a fox.

A. A lion falls into traps, and a fox cannot escape a wolf.

B. A prince should not keep his word when it will do him harm.

C. Although it is important to appear to be honest, princes often have to deceive.

D. In this discussion, Machiavelli tells his readers that results must be kept in mind when evaluating a prince.

E. Often, this passage is translated as "the ends justify the means," but that is not quite accurate.

IV. One of the prince's greatest fears is a conspiracy against him.

A. Machiavelli will deal much more thoroughly with conspiracies in his *Florentine Histories* (see Lecture Twenty-Two).

B. Here, however, he states that conspiracies are difficult to carry out because of the fact that more than one person is involved.

C. The best way for a prince not to fall prey to conspiracies is to have the people on his side.

V. In chapter 19, Machiavelli examines institutions and practices of France and the Roman Empire.

A. He likes the French Parlement, a judicial body that restrains the nobles.

B. Because the French king does not control the Parlement, he can avoid being hated by the nobles.

C. Machiavelli looks at several Roman emperors of the late 2nd and 3rd centuries, explaining why some succeeded while others failed.

    1. He praises Septimius Severus for playing well the roles of lion and fox.

    2. The other emperors he discusses did not succeed, often because of their cruelty.

D. Machiavelli recognizes that rulers in his time have somewhat different problems than those ancient emperors and explains how one can and cannot borrow directly from the past.

E. Machiavelli pronounces that in his time, it is more important for princes to satisfy the people rather than their soldiers, but he says that the Ottoman emperor is an exception to this rule.

VI. Machiavelli takes up military tactics a prince needs to employ.

A. Generally, princes leave their subjects armed or arm them themselves.

B. The exception is when a prince annexes an adjacent territory; then, he should disarm all but his supporters.

C. Machiavelli examines the traditional Florentine tactic of holding Pisa by means of fortresses and Pistoia by means of factions.

    1. This strategy may have been good policy when there was a balance of power in Italy from 1454 to 1494.

    2. It is a bad tactic in the present.

D. On the matter of building fortresses, Machiavelli argues that it depends on the situation.

    1. A prince should build fortresses if he fears his own people more than foreigners.

    2. The best fortress consists of not being hated by the people.

Recommended Readings:

Machiavelli, *The Prince*, translated by Peter Bondanella, chapters 17–21.

Questions to Consider:

1. Is being feared really safer than being loved?

2. How are the skills of the lion and the fox complementary rather than contradictory?

3. What are ways that princes can win the esteem and admiration of those whom they govern?

Lecture Ten—Transcript
The Prince, 17–21—The Lion and the Fox

Our next topic in doing our "text-crawling" through *The Prince* is to look at an important moral principle of a leader. A leader should be merciful. Machiavelli said, yeah, a leader should be thought merciful, but we've got think about what it means to be merciful. Sometimes we assume we know what merciful means and what cruel means, and we may get that wrong. So yes, mercy is a good thing; let's talk about what mercy really means.

Once again—this should not surprise anybody by now—he comes back to Cesare Borgia. Let me read you a passage that he wrote about Cesare Borgia in this context. Remember again that Cesare took over the Romagna; it was a mess. It was chaotic, he sent in this tough guy Ramiro d'Orco to really shape up the Romagna and he was cruel, and he was cruel with the approval and knowledge of Cesare Borgia. Then, as Cesare Borgia realized that he didn't want to be seen as being this really heavy-handed nasty guy, he cut him in half and propped him up in a piazza in the city of Cesana to send the message to the people, hey, I don't approve of all that stuff that's gone on. Now, that sounds pretty cruel in a couple of different ways; let's see how Machiavelli analyzes it in the context of cruelty and mercy. "Turning to the other qualities mentioned above, let me say that every prince must be desire to be considered merciful and not cruel. Nevertheless, he must take care not to use such mercy badly. Cesare Borgia was considered cruel, nonetheless, this cruelty of his brought order to the Romagna, united it, and restored it to peace and loyalty. If we examine this carefully, we shall see that he was more merciful than the Florentine people who allowed the destruction of Pistoia, in order to avoid being considered cruel."

Okay, let's take this apart. Cesare Borgia heavy handed by using Ramiro d'Orco to do a lot of cruel things to bring, we would say today, law and order to the Romagna. Then, Cesare Borgia slices him up to say, hey, I'm not sure I approved of all that. I didn't know about all this stuff, when of course Cesare Borgia did. Now, what's the result of all this? A) Ramiro d'Orco's dead, we'll start with that. B) the Romagna is ordered. People obey the law because they think that bad things will happen to them if they disobey the law and they might actually get caught now. Because Cesare, through Ramiro and through others, has been able to restore order, some sort of stability. Giovanni the farmer can now bring his crops into town, sell them, go back home, and not expect to be mugged on the road. That's one example.

Then, he uses the example of Florence. When Machiavelli was a secretary of the Florentine republic—and this is, by the way, not just from Machiavelli's time, but it's all through Florentine history—the city of Pistoia, a little bit to the west toward Pisa, part of the Florentine state, was bitterly, bitterly divided by factions. In fact, you go all the way back to the end of the 13th century and that's where the Black and White Guelf split started with a quarrel in Pistoia. So, Pistoia is tearing itself apart through factions. What do the Florentines do? They do nothing because to go in and tromp on this and stop this factional feuding, the Florentines were afraid that people were going to say, "Ooh, ooh, those Florentines are cruel." Now, what's the result of that? The result of that is a lot of people in Pistoia are getting killed in these bitter and violent factional struggles.

Now, who's cruel and who is merciful? That's the question that Machiavelli asks. Traditionally, you would say Cesare Borgia was cruel and the Florentines were merciful because they didn't jump on anybody. They didn't throw anybody in jail. They didn't beat up anybody in Pistoia to put down those disturbances. But, who is really merciful? Is it the guy who left the Romagna relatively stable and peaceful, although he did it by means of cruelty? Or, is it the Florentines who sought to be thought of as merciful and, as a result, people are getting their throats slit and their heads clunked all the time in the streets of Pistoia? Now, who is really cruel and who is really merciful? That's the question that Machiavelli wants to ask. He's saying it's not so simple as you might think. It's not a matter of looking up in the dictionary a traditional definition of cruel and a traditional definition of mercy and then assigning those to the Florentines or to Cesare Borgia. It's more difficult than that. There needs to be a different perspective taken in terms of what are the results—not just what are the tools that were used in forging a policy, in forging a way of governance.

So, Machiavelli's at his most challenging to us here because I think most people are, I hope, rightly put off with the idea of simply going in and probably not paying much attention to what we call human rights or civil rights, as Cesare Borgia did in the Romagna. And yet, the Romagna turns out to get pretty well governed after a time of chaos. On the other hand, probably we would tend today to say, well

I'm glad the Florentines didn't go into Pistoia and knock a lot of heads, that's never good policy. Machiavelli at least makes us think about this in a somewhat different way and says change your perspective. Don't go by those dictionary definitions—which in his day meant the definitions of Aristotle or Cicero or whoever it might be—but look at it from a different perspective, re-conceptualize it, and see if you come to the same conclusion or to a different conclusion.

From there, Machiavelli turns to a related question and that is, is it better to be feared or to be loved? Cicero had said loved because if you are loved by your constituents—not a very good word but—if you're loved by those whom you govern, then you'll be okay. You don't have anything to fear. Now, Machiavelli says, let's face it, the best thing is to be both feared and loved. Okay, let's take the best of both worlds if we can get it. But, he says, if you can only have one, it is better to be feared than loved and the reason is we need to understand the way humans really are. People are fickle. People are deceptive. Men will more likely attack someone they love, but don't fear than vice versa. And we can sort of see where Machiavelli's coming from.

Let's say that somebody tries to recruit me for some sort of rebellion, for some sort of attempt to change things by popular force. In what situation am I more likely to go along with people who were persuading me to join? A) I sort of like my prince. He's a nice guy. He throws a nice festival now and then. I love him. Well, we know that love can be pretty fickle; if you don't think so, you pay no attention to public opinion polls. We know that love can be very, very fickle. Again, any president can tell you all about those very big ups and downs in approval ratings and so on. Or, B) am I likely to go into some sort of struggle against my prince if I really fear him, saying I'm going to get caught and if I get caught, he's going to do some bad things to me. I'm going to spend time in jail or get a hand lopped off or get a head lopped off or whatever it might be. Which situation, fear or love, makes me more likely or less likely to enter into some sort of activity or conspiracy against my prince? It is better to be feared than loved.

However, Machiavelli, goes on next to say—and this is a very important distinction he makes—it is vital that princes avoid being hated. Being feared and being hated are not the same thing, and princes must not be hated. Now, here's the easiest way not to be hated; don't take people's property and don't take people's women. Machiavelli says if you do that—remember that we're primarily talking about new principalities, go all the way back to that scheme that Machiavelli laid out of the kinds of governments we're going to talk about. We saw there were different kinds of principalities; we're primarily interested in new principalities. You'll come in and take over some place like Cesare Borgia did, you might bash a few heads; what you don't do is you don't tax them a lot and you don't take their women for yourself or your soldiers or whatever it might be. You need to avoid being hated and those are the primary ways you'll end up being hated.

I think, at this point, Machiavelli introduces one of the most interesting and evocative examples that he gives from the ancient world. It comes from Livy, although not the part of Livy he's going to write his discourses on. He only writes his discourses on the very early history of Rome according to Livy. This is an example that comes from the second Punic War and the example is Hannibal, the guy who crossed the Alps and all that sort of stuff. Machiavelli says this: "Historians have always praised Hannibal because Hannibal kept his army in Italy," in a foreign land, "disciplined and loyal for many years." This war went on for close to 20 years and for most of that time, Hannibal and his men were away from Carthage and in Italy, loyal and disciplined all that time. Historians say, "What a great general Hannibal was because he was able to do that." Then historians say, "There's one bad thing about Hannibal. We may praise him for the loyalty and whatever of his troops and keeping all that, but there's one thing we don't praise him for. There's one thing we condemn him for and that is he was inhumanly cruel."

Wait a minute, Machiavelli says, you can't praise one and condemn the other, when in fact they're intimately related. Why did Hannibal's army remain loyal and disciplined? Answer—because he was inhumanly cruel; because if you weren't disciplined and orderly and loyal, you're going to end up without a limb or a head or some other such part of your body. Such was the way Hannibal kept order in a foreign land with his army all of those years. You know, presumably, Hannibal's soldiers like everybody else, they sort of like to go home, see the wife and the kids, to stroll the familiar streets, to get back into that pattern of life that they have lived. But no, they're with Hannibal all this time. How did Hannibal keep them in line? Not by stroking them, not by saying come on guys, let's play cards tonight; he did it by his cruelty. The point Machiavelli makes is that so often when we analyze the past or the present for that matter, we praise and blame certain things, not realizing what the inter-relationship is. If you're going to praise Hannibal, you've got to accept that the cruelty is what led to his success as an organizer and leader of men. If you're going to criticize Hannibal, say he's a bad guy, then you've got to realize that those things he did that you don't like led to a good result; the result was an ordered and disciplined army that was able to fight in the field for years against the Romans on Roman territory.

And so, Machiavelli is saying, very often, we're naïve. Oh that Hannibal—great general, nasty guy. He was a great general, in a sense, because he was a nasty guy. And, we have to put the pieces together and we can't divorce them. This is a very important lesson Machiavelli wants to teach us about the way we not just analyze the past, but also analyze the present. Hannibal was feared by his soldiers; he wasn't hated, but he was feared by his soldiers and to obtain that fear, he had to do some pretty tough, nasty things. That's the way it goes, Machiavelli again. Remember, this sort of new political science we're talking about is a political science that's interested in what is, rather than what should be. What should be is somebody else's task; Machiavelli's task is to talk about what is.

Then, Machiavelli turns to perhaps the most famous image that he gives us in *The Prince*, although it's not an image that he himself invents. Let me read to you from Chapter 18: "Since then a prince must know how to make use of the nature of the beast," animals, "he should choose from among the beasts the fox and the lion, for the lion cannot defend itself from traps while the fox cannot protect itself from the wolves. It is therefore necessary to be a fox in order to recognize the traps and a lion in order to frighten the wolves. Those who base their behavior only on the lion do not understand things, a wise ruler therefore cannot and should not keep his word when such an observance would be to his disadvantage." Now, the image of the lion and the fox is, as I said, older than Machiavelli. But, what we want to see is Machiavelli is saying, a prince needs to be strong and tough and thoughtful and clever. It's not either, or. There's a famous character in Dante's *Inferno* who says, "I was like the fox, rather than the lion." I was a cunning guy is what he was saying. By the way, again, Machiavelli knows Dante very well, talks about reading Dante all the time and occasionally quotes him.

But here, what Machiavelli says is, you need to be both. You need cunning and cleverness and insight, and you need strength. There are times when you need to roar and there are times when you need to sneak about, and you've got to do not one or the other, but both. It's important to be honest, but it's important to know how to deceive and to deceive when necessary. It's in the context of talking about the roles of the prince, in terms of lion and fox, that Machiavelli makes one of his most quoted or perhaps, it's fair to say, misquoted statements. Let me read it to you; it's very brief. "In the actions of all men, and especially of princes, where there is no tribunal to which to appeal one must consider the final results." Now, the way that is often translated is that the ends justify the means. If there's one phrase today we probably associate with Machiavelli, it's that one. He never said those words. That is not to say that this is an idea foreign to Machiavelli, but we need to remember that words matter. It matters whether he says those exact words or some other words that we interpret that way. It's important to understand what Machiavelli says. We need to keep in mind the goal, and we need to act accordingly to achieve that goal.

Now, of course, this leads to a question, is this true for any old goal or must the goal be a right goal and how do we define the goal? Machiavelli doesn't go into that here. What Machiavelli says is, assuming a prince is seeking to bring order and stability and security to the territory he rules, then he must always keep that in mind when deciding whether or not he's going to be cruel, whether or not he's going to be honest, because to act on those specific matters without saying is this going to help or hinder me in achieving my goal, is fruitless. It won't work. It won't get you anywhere. It won't lead to success. Cesare Borgia, in a sense, knew what he wanted, and then he figured out what he would have to do—sometimes pretty ugly things— what he would have to do to achieve it. But Machiavelli would say Cesare was always on message. Here's what I want to achieve—how do I treat the people in the Romagna? How do I treat the thieves we catch? How do I treat my minister Ramiro d'Orco? I treat him in the way that will get me to my goal and I'll have to make a judgment as to what that is. I can reward him or I can slice him in half. In this case, of course, we know that Cesare sliced Ramiro d'Orco in half.

But, Machiavelli says you've got to think about the goal because without that in mind, you're just sort of floundering. You're sort of guessing. You're sort of operating in a piecemeal way, rather than having some sort of integrated plan as prince. This is a very important point that Machiavelli makes; does this translate to the ends justify the means? Since those are, again, not exactly his words, it's something we can debate. Certainly, he's saying something close to that, but the words we need to focus on are, you always have to keep the goal in mind. Again, for Machiavelli, the goal of the prince—I said this 74 times, why not say it the 75th time—the goal of a prince is to create an orderly, stable, secure state. So, how do you do it? As you know from Machiavelli's time to our time, we debate whether or not using certain unpleasant means, by their definition, damage a good goal or whether they are, in fact, a means to achieving a good goal. It's one we can and we should debate. We don't have to take Machiavelli's side at all. What we need to say is Machiavelli has framed the issue for us in a way that's useful for us to make use of. It's useful for us to use Machiavelli's way of stating things because it will help us think through things carefully.

Machiavelli talks about the problem of conspiracies in a political society. There are always going to be conspiracies. There are always going to be people plotting behind the backs of others, in private, to get rid of or to modify the behavior of a prince. Conspiracies go with the territory. Now, Machiavelli doesn't spend a lot of time on conspiracies here. He's going to spend a lot more time talking about conspiracies in *The Florentine Histories*, where he's going to focus in and give us a detailed account of the conspiracy against the Medici in 1478, the so-called Pazzi Conspiracy. But, here, just take these points of Machiavelli; conspiracies are difficult to carry out because there's always, by definition, more than one person involved. When there is a conspiracy, it really helps to have the people on your side. Again, there are going to be conspiracies. If one is attempted, you really need the people to come to your defense, which is exactly what happens when one of the two Medici brothers was killed in 1478. The people rounded up the folks that they thought were responsible and demanded that they be hanged, cut up in little pieces, and thrown in the Arno River, so that nobody would sort of hold on to the pieces of their body or remember them.

Continuing with this notion of being feared, but not being hated, Machiavelli looks at some of the ways that societies outside Italy, now, and ancient societies have had successful rulers who were perhaps cruel and feared, but were not hated. He looks at one institution that he learned about when he was a diplomat in France, the Parliament, as it's called in France. Now, we hear that word and we say that sounds like parliament to us, it must be a legislative body; not at all. The Parliament, and especially the Parliament in Paris, were judicial bodies and their job, really, in large part was to restrain the nobles. This was a brilliant institution, Machiavelli says, because nobles don't like being restrained. Nobles are not going to like people who restrain them and so the king doesn't have to do it because there's an institution that does it, the Parliament, which is essentially independent, at least in theory, of the French monarchy. And so, this is one of those things he learns as a diplomat from his experience being in France and says what a good idea, because the result is the king of France can sort of get his way, to some extent, with a limited nobility, without him being the guy that does the limiting. Now there's an institution Machiavelli likes.

Machiavelli also takes a look at several of the Roman Emperors, especially in the 2nd and 3rd centuries A.D., when the Roman Empire was fairly chaotic after the death of Marcus Aurelius. He praises the emperor Septimius Severus—some of you may know Septimius Severus, a 3rd-century emperor because at one end of the Roman forum that you visit today in Rome is the biggest triumphal arch of Septimius Severus; at the other end is the arch of Titus, you may recall. Machiavelli praises Septimius Severus because he says he was both a lion and a fox; he got the lion-fox thing and he did that well. He said the other emperors of that era—and, by the way, it seemed like there was almost an emperor a year during this period of Roman history—did not succeed because they did their cruelty in such a way that they were hated. If you will, it was too much lion, not very much fox. And so, Machiavelli looks around and draws from different kinds of experiences—the modern French monarchy, the ancient Roman Empire—to take a look at ways that you can succeed in being tough without being hated and ways in which people have tried and failed.

Therefore, Machiavelli says, what do we do with all of this stuff? The bottom line is that today, whether it's in France or whether it's in Florence, rulers have a different set of circumstances than Septimius Severus had or, for that matter, in Italy, than the king of France has in his own day; therefore, it makes it difficult to borrow directly from the past. You can't just say Septimius Severus was a successful emperor, I'll do exactly what he did, and this is a point Machiavelli's going to make over and over and over. In all the books of his that we're examining and in those we aren't examining, for that matter, how do you use the past? How do you use it intelligently and creatively? You don't Xerox the past and make it the present.

You have to figure out how to adapt the success of the past so you will be successful in a somewhat different set of circumstances.

Now, for example, Machiavelli says let me give you a general rule today. I look around Italy, I look around France, I look around Germany, and I look around Spain. Let me give you a general rule of how princes need to act today. Princes need to satisfy the people more than they need to satisfy their soldiers. Satisfying the people is more important than satisfying the soldiers, but there's an exception to that. Remember that for the last—well, from 1453 on—for the last 60–70 years, the city of Constantinople, much of what we call Turkey today, and much of what we call the Balkans today were being ruled by the Ottoman Turks. And, he says the exception is the Ottoman Empire. He's very interested in the Ottoman Empire. By the way, he never makes a comment about different religions or they come from a different religious tradition. He simply says I'm going to look at the political realities in the Ottoman Empire. And, the political realities of the Ottoman Empire, he says, are that the Ottoman Emperors need to satisfy the soldiers first and the people second, the opposite of France or various states in Italy or Germany or Spain or whatever it might be. There is no hard and fast rule. You can't write the rules down. You've got to look at the circumstances, look at past examples, and adapt them to your circumstances. History being useful is a very a creative process, Machiavelli points out.

Let me turn to another topic now. Machiavelli discusses military tactics and he says some things that perhaps surprise us. He says when princes conquer new territories, they either leave their subjects armed or they arm them. You've got to win the people to be on your side, or you're not going to make it anyway, we've seen why for a number of reasons and, therefore, we want those people armed. If they aren't armed, you arm them. Now, Machiavelli says once again, we're talking about how he uses history, there's an exception to this rule. The exception is if you conquer a territory adjacent to your own, then you have to disarm the people you conquer because, of course, they can use those arms and attack you since you're their neighbors—that is to say, the place from which you came. So again, there are rules, but those rules have to be read flexibly and in context. There are no hard and fast rules. There are no shortcuts. There are no, memorize these 12 principles and you will be a successful prince. You need to be a lion and a fox and foxes are clever and foxes move around and they make adjustments. That's what foxes do; that's what a prince needs to do as well.

Machiavelli turns to one particular example of how historical circumstances change. He says this has always been the motto in Florence, you hold Pisa by fortresses, and you hold Pistoia by factions. Now, Machiavelli really isn't crazy about that idea, but he said it might have been a reasonable way to hold Pisa and Pistoia during the period of 40 years between 1454 and 1494, when generally speaking, there was a balance of power in Italy. It might have made sense under those circumstances, when Italy was relatively peaceful and the five major states were sort of in a kind of balance, but it certainly doesn't make any sense to continue that policy after that 40 years of relative peace broke down with the invasion of the French in 1494. And, then, Machiavelli asks this question; should you build fortresses? Well, it's an interesting answer that he has—a prince should build fortresses if he fears his own people more than foreigners. Fortresses are not about hiding in when you're invaded; fortresses are about hiding in when there's rebellion around you. So, if you don't trust the people and you think they hate you build fortresses but the best fortresses Machiavelli says, very interesting, the best fortresses are the people not hating you. That is your real safety within your city-state.

Lecture Eleven
The Prince, 21–26—Fortune and Foreigners

Scope:

Machiavelli explains how a prince must gain the esteem of his people. He then addresses several important issues regarding a prince's court. One concerns advisors and how princes use them. Another is the problem of flattery. I will discuss how Machiavelli treats these two matters.

Finally, Machiavelli focuses once again on contemporary Italy and its problems, most of which were, in a sense, self-inflicted. He asks if these problems are simply caused by Fortune. Although Machiavelli recognizes the role of Fortune, he also counsels how to mitigate her control over human affairs.

Since 1494, Italy has seen invading armies from north of the Alps. In the last chapter of *The Prince*, Machiavelli famously presents a passionate exhortation for Italy to be freed from "the barbarians." This passage was often cited during the age of Italian unification in the 19th century and made Machiavelli, along with Dante, the prophet of a united Italian state.

Outline

I. Princes need the esteem of their people.

   A. The king of Spain showed himself to be extraordinary by expelling the Muslims and attacking Italy.

   B. It is better for a prince to be a true friend or a true enemy than to remain neutral.

   C. A prince needs to take risks.

   D. A prince should honor great men and sponsor spectacles.

   E. Princes need to recognize the importance of community and local organizations, such as guilds and neighborhoods.

II. Princes are judged by the men who serve them.

   A. Machiavelli praises Pandolfo Petrucci of Siena, who was well regarded for having such a good minister.

   B. A man who puts his own interests first will not make a good minister.

C. A prince should make his chief ministers rich so that they think they cannot do as well without the prince.

III. Flattery is a serious problem at courts.

    A. The prince should tell his ministers that he wants to hear the truth.

    B. However, the prince needs to make clear that this is true only of those men and only when he asks for it, which should be often.

    C. A prince should ask frequent questions about everything and be a good listener.

IV. Machiavelli examines princes who have lost their states and asks why.

    A. Some had the people turn against them.

    B. Others did not know how to control the nobles.

    C. When a prince who has ruled for a long time loses his state, the loss is due to his errors and not to Fortune.

V. An oft-discussed question is the role of Fortune in worldly affairs, and Machiavelli makes this the final topic in *The Prince*.

    A. Machiavelli thinks that Fortune is about half responsible for matters of state.

        1. Fortune is like a river that overflows and destroys.

        2. The river cannot really be controlled.

        3. However, if one takes advance precautions, one can lessen the damage the river causes.

    B. Given that Fortune is a woman, it is generally better to be bold than cautious when dealing with her.

    C. What matters most for success is for a prince to adapt himself to the circumstances.

        1. In some situations, it is best to be cautious, while in others, one must be bold to succeed.

        2. He adds, however, that it is almost impossible for one kind of prince to act counter to his own character.

        3. An example is Pope Julius II, whose impetuous character was exactly what was needed while he was pope.

        4. Had Julius lived at a time requiring caution, he would not have been successful.

VI. Machiavelli concludes *The Prince* with an exhortation to the Medici to drive foreigners out of Italy.

    A. Italy had suffered a number of foreign armies on its soil beginning in 1494, but the situation at the time *The Prince* was written saw circumstances favorable to expelling them.

    B. Machiavelli probably had seen Cesare Borgia as a potential liberator of Italy.

    C. Given that members of the Medici family rule two of the five major states in Italy (Florence and the papacy), they should become the leaders of Italy's liberation.

        1. Machiavelli sees signs in nature to indicate the success the Medici will have.

        2. These signs parallel those in Egypt at the time of the Exodus of the Hebrews.

        3. Machiavelli urges the Medici to create an army of their own rather than to rely on mercenaries.

            a. The Spanish soldiers cannot defeat cavalry.

            b. The Swiss infantry is not invincible.

    D. Machiavelli ends with patriotic fervor and quotes a passage from Petrarch that says that ancient valor is not dead in Italy.

Recommended Readings:

Machiavelli, *The Prince*, translated by Peter Bondanella, chapters 21–26.

Questions to Consider:

1. Why is the wise choice and proper use of advisors centrally important to a prince's success?

2. To what extent do we control our situations, and to what extent are we products of matters we cannot control?

3. Is Machiavelli the great Italian nationalist he was made out to be during the Risorgimento in the 19th century?

Lecture Eleven—Transcript
The Prince, 21–26—Fortune and Foreigners

We've been talking for a while about the prince needing not to be hated. I'm going to take up a topic briefly that's a positive rather than a negative quality the princes need. Princes need the esteem of their people. It isn't so much being liked or loved; it's being, in a sense, respected because of some great things that the prince has done. So, for example, Machiavelli says, the King of Spain is esteemed because he showed himself to be an extraordinary king by expelling the Muslims and by attacking Italy. You do big things if you are a prince because big things get the attention and a kind of respect from people. He gives a somewhat more pedestrian example, too. He says that people will esteem you and respect you if they have no fear of confiscation of their property or increase in their taxes. He also says it's better for a prince to be a true friend or a true enemy than to remain neutral.

Machiavelli wants to make a point and he will make it again and again in the last part of *The Prince*. Basically, the job of prince is not compatible with being a wimp. That if you're going to be a prince, you need to do some bold things. It's good to have friends and it's good to have enemies, or at least it's okay to have enemies; what you don't want is everybody going blah. This person doesn't stand for anything. This person isn't a friend to anybody or an enemy to everybody. You don't try to please everybody all the time. He really emphasizes the boldness of princely activity. That means princes should take risks. Being a prince does not mean playing it safe, but that it's important to take risks. Those who just sort of try to ride along and not cause any trouble, not upset anybody, have 100% approval ratings—those folks, Machiavelli thinks will fail while somebody who has some friends and some enemies, who tries bold things, maybe not all of which work perfectly—those folks will be better off.

One last point in terms of gaining esteem—Machiavelli says that princes need to honor great citizens. You aren't jealous of people in your principality that do great deeds. You honor them. You respect them. You give them a medal. You put up a statue or whatever it might be. And also, Machiavelli says, it's important to put on spectacles. Now, God knows Florence had spectacles and nobody was better than the Medici, for example, in really making sure that on the feast day of Florence's patron saint, who is John the Baptist, the date is the 24th of June, even to this day by the way, the Florentines really put on a spectacle. There were plays, there were concerts, there were jousts in the main square; there was a parade that involved various organizations, guilds, confraternities of the bishop, everybody. And, the Medici spent a great deal of money on all this. That there is a kind of pageantry that's important. A lot of scholars have written about this in modern times, the importance of ritual. And the Florentines, especially the Medici, were very, very good at this. If any of you've had a chance to go to Italy, especially if you've had a chance to go to Florence's southern neighbor, Siena, you may know that twice a year, Siena still has this huge spectacle that culminates in a horse race called the Palio. I'm there virtually every year and although it's exciting and tourists like all the flag-waving and all this sort of stuff, it really is a ritual where in the parade around the central square before the horse race the whole city of Siena is, in fact, its history is reenacted and various costumes and what we would call floats today, are things that remind the Sienese of the great markers in their history. It's important to have those things, Machiavelli says. Honor great men and sponsor spectacles.

And Machiavelli also says we need to remember that not only do people identify themselves as citizens, but they also identify themselves as members of neighborhoods, members of guilds, members of, if you will, more local organizations, all of which have their own rituals and spectacles and activities and dinners and patron saints and whatever. And, Machiavelli says, a good prince visits those. A good prince let's people know he cares about those local organizations. We know how it is today in the United States; there are so many people who feel such deep loyalty to their neighborhood, to their parish, to their social organization, to their labor union, and Machiavelli says princes need to recognize those things. If you will, the kind of esteem and comfort and respect that citizens have for their prince doesn't begin with things that are princedom-wide, but begins with smaller units of that society and sort of culminates in, for example, a great festival where all the guilds have their floats, all the guilds march in the parade and show not just who they are as individuals or small groups, but that they're also part of that whole. So, Machiavelli emphasizes some of these positive ways that princes can and should gain the esteem of their citizens.

Another important topic that Machiavelli takes up is who serves a prince, his ministers; we would say today, I suppose, in a modern

American term, his cabinet—his inner circle of advisors. Princes, Machiavelli says, are judged by the men who serve them and, in fact, Machiavelli singles out an older contemporary of his named Pandolfo Petrucci who was, more or less, the Prince of Siena. Siena was on paper a republic, but it wasn't always a republic any more than Florence always was. And, he says, Petrucci was well regarded because he had such a good—we would say today—prime minister. That is important that those folks be the folks that gain you esteem and respect. Now, what makes a good minister and how do you get them?

First of all, a good minister is one who puts the prince's interests first and not his own. You don't want to hire a careerist, if you will, as your minister: somebody who's interested in his own honor or glory. You need to have somebody who genuinely cares about and recognizes that this is all about the prince and not himself, or today him or herself. Machiavelli also says ministers ought to be very well paid because you want people serving you who say, "Gosh, if I do anything to fall out of favor with this prince, if I do something behind his back and I get fired, I'm going to be a lot less well off than I am now." You want to reward your ministers so that they recognize from their own personal perspective how necessary it is for them to be loyal to you. Now, Machiavelli knows that one of the greatest problems at the court of a prince is flattery. Dante has said this; we know that at the end of the 16th century, people like Shakespeare are going to say that. Machiavelli's contemporary Thomas Moore writes about flattery in his book *Utopia*, which by the way was written about three years after *The Prince*. Flattery is a problem. You've got to have ministers who are A) under your control, but B) tell you the truth.

How do you do that? First of all, the prince says to his ministers, I want you to tell me the truth, knowing that sometimes that's not what the prince wants to hear; telling the truth is an important thing. Let me read this passage, from Machiavelli, this is Chapter 23: "Therefore, a prudent prince should follow this course, electing wise men for his state and giving only them permission to speak truthfully to him and only such matters as he asks them about and not on other subjects. But, he should ask them about everything and should listen to their opinions. And afterward he should deliberate by himself in his own way and in such councils and with each of his ministers he should conduct himself in such a way that all will realize that the more freely they speak, the more they will please him. Apart from these, he should refuse to listen to anyone else."

It's interesting because sometimes I think we only hear part of what Machiavelli says. Machiavelli says okay you guys, a particular group of ministers, or the prime minister, whoever it is, you tell me the truth. Don't volunteer it, it's only when I ask you and what I ask you about. Now, that part is often quoted, often quoted. We know that sometimes that could lead to people ultimately still hearing what they want to hear. But notice what Machiavelli says right after that, "But you should ask them about everything." The people you trust, you ask them about everything. It's important that you hear what people think or that your own reasoning is flawed, and so it's not just saying I don't want to hear everything from everybody. I want to focus it on people whom I've chosen, whom I respect, whom I know are ultimately on my side—your ministers. But, tell it like it is. Be as frank and as honest, and to the prince, Machiavelli says, ask them about everything—not just a few things—everything. In fact, Machiavelli follows up the passage I read by saying that a prince needs to be a frequent questioner and a good listener. So, Machiavelli understands the necessity for a prince to choose ministers well, to treat them in a certain way, and to know what the job of a minister is. It's important for the prince to know what the job of a minister is; it's important for the ministers to know what the job of the minister is so there's no misunderstanding, so there's no confusion.

I'm reminded when I think about this of a book out by Doris Kearns Goodwin about Abraham Lincoln and his cabinet. I talked to her about this as she was writing the book and one of the points she make is, the very people who challenged Lincoln for the nomination, people who were much better educated than Lincoln, he brought all those people into his cabinet, whether it was William Seward or others, and that became so important for the way the Lincoln presidency succeeded and it had all of its brilliant successes. That's important, to have the right ministers, for you to know who you are, and for them to know who they are. And, to have all of that laid out, and then you can get the advice you need without being distracted by a lot of extraneous matter. So, if we listen to the whole of what Machiavelli says about this, as opposed to listening to a little snippet of what Machiavelli says about this, it seems to me that there's some wisdom here that we need to consider.

Machiavelli briefly asks, why have certain princes lost the states that they once held, that they once controlled? Well, here are some answers. Machiavelli says, first of all—and you should not be surprised that this is first—the people turn against a prince. He ends up being hated or he ends up being loved, but not feared; we talked about these things. These will lead to a prince losing his principality. You cannot afford to have the people turn against you; remember what he said that I mentioned at the end of last lecture. The support of the people is the best fortress you can have. It's the best protection you can have within your own territory. A second problem the princes have is that many who've lost their kingdom did not know how to control the nobility. We need to remember the nobility were, after all, a group set aside, legally privileged. In many cases, the nobility, of course, is a hereditary nobility; they trace their lineage back far beyond where anybody really could and all you know, all of the sudden, they've been there since the beginning or their families have been there since the beginning or they're related to gods or all kinds of crazy stuff that you get. Well, you've got to be able to control the nobility. You can't let them control you because, again, a point Machiavelli made earlier in *The Prince*, a lot of nobility think they're as a good as you are. They think they're your equal and you've got to find ways to control them; you're not going to eliminate them, but if you don't control them, if you allow them to get out of control, then you might lose your territory.

Machiavelli says, by the way, if you've been prince a long time and you lose your territory, it's your fault. After all, we know that when princes become princes, sometimes things are so delicate that something out of their control can happen and change things so much that they lose power. But, if a prince has been around for a while and has acted wisely as a prince, he will not lose his principality. If he does, it's because he has not followed, among other things, the advice that Machiavelli gives in *The Prince*.

Machiavelli then turns, as his final topic in *The Prince* before his last flourish of a conclusion, to the issue of fortune. Now, you see how this fits with where we just came from. That is to say, to what extent do things happen to us over which we have no control that really determine how things go? Whether it's an earthquake or a flood or a bad crop or whatever it might be, somebody dying at an unexpected time, and throwing all of our plans awry. How do we understand fortune and its role? Machiavelli says I think fortune is about 50% of it. Let me read you again one of the famous passages from *The Prince* about fortune: "Fortune is the arbiter of one-half of our actions, but that she still leaves us to control the other half, or almost to us, that I want to assert." He continues, "I compare her to one of those destructive rivers that when they become enraged, flood the plains, ruin the trees and buildings, raising the earth from one spot and dropping it on to another. Everyone flees before it, everyone yields to its impetus, unable to oppose it in any way, but although rivers are like this, it does not mean that we cannot take precautions with dikes and dams when the weather is calm so that when they rise up again either the waters will be channeled off or their force will neither be so damaging nor so out of control. The same things occur where fortune is concerned. She shows her power where there is no well ordered virtue," think about the meaning of that word, "to resist her and, therefore, turns her impetus towards where she knows no dikes and dams have been constructed to hold her in." This is a very interesting passage.

Remember, we saw this applied to a specific issue and now generalized. How do you get ready for war? You do it in times of peace because when war comes, there's no time for all that studying, there's no time for all that planning, all that strategizing, all that discussion, all that imagination at work. In general, fortune is like a river. I remember the famous flood in Florence in 1966 that did so much destruction to the art. Well, let's talk about that as a modern analog to what Machiavelli is saying. There were extraordinary rains in the area above Florence where the Arno forms, and that's out of our control. We have no control over how much it rains up in the Cosentino, as that area is called, but of course Florence wasn't prepared for so much water. And, when the water came into Florence, it overflowed the banks of the Arno and did so much destruction. Now today if that storm came, it would do much, much less damage because I think the Florentines, the Italians, have learned their lesson, and now they're ready. There are more ways to deal with that magnitude of water, which could come, and over which there is no control. And so, what we have to do is think ahead and plan and you plan for worse-case scenarios. You plan for disasters that you have no control over. What are you going to do if the crop doesn't come in this year? What are you going to do if the Arno floods? What are you going to do if there's no rain this year? What are you going to do if your leader dies at the height of his power with nobody ever thinking that he won't live another 20 years? What do you do? You have to plan. Fortune is a river; you can't control what goes into the river, but you can control how much damage it does. That's the way, Machiavelli says, you have to think.

Now, he also says, by the way, that using an ancient line that fortune is a woman. After all, remember in a gendered language, we have the situation that *Fortuna*, the Latin and the Italian words based on it, are feminine. Fortune is a woman and Machiavelli says that you know it is better to be bold than cautious because it's better to be bold than cautious with women. Now, all of this discussion of fortune leads to Machiavelli talking about the fact that, well, we have to be prepared to adapt to circumstances. We have to be flexible. Sometimes it's better to be cautious. Sometimes it's better to be bold and you have to know which is which. You have to have, in a sense, thoughts about various kinds of contingencies. If this happens, that is the appropriate response, but if this doesn't happen, we respond very differently. And so, there's this constant sense and it goes back to the way Machiavelli says we use history, we use it creatively. We don't copy the past. We incorporate the lessons of the past into our present, which might mean the situation that we're looking at here may call on a different action than what seems to be a parallel situation in the past because the past has always inexact parallels at best. Analogies are, after all, not equal; there are similarities, as well as dissimilarities. We have to think about all that and make sure we know how to use a lesson from the past or from another country, as in the case of France or whatever it might be.

Now, here's the problem, Machiavelli says. The problem is most princes, most people, have a certain character. Some people are just, it seems, cautious by nature. Others are bold or even reckless by nature and if we are one of those things by nature, it is very hard to become something else. It's very hard to change. Only the greatest princes, I think Machiavelli suggests, really can do that. I always think of the analogy of coaches of sports. It seems to me that the coaches that succeed in basketball or football are the ones that say, this is the kind of offense I prefer, but I don't have the right quarterback or I don't have the right combination of players to play that offense that I think is the best offense in principle. Well, as you know, what happens—a coach has a couple choices. You can play that offense anyway, or you can say I've got to adapt to my personnel and play a somewhat different offense than I would if I were completely in charge of who my personnel were and what their qualities were. And, Machiavelli would say, it's that coach who succeeds, it's that prince who succeeds, but it's a very rare quality to be able to really change; for somebody bold to be able to say, oh time for caution or vice versa. Machiavelli recognizes this.

He talks about, for example, Pope Julius II—again pope during the first decade of the 16th century. He says Julius II was impetuous and that's exactly the kind of pope who was needed, given the needs of the territory he governed, the Papal States, and the situation of the surrounding territories at that time. And so, Julius II was successful politically and militarily because his impetuosity was needed at that time. But, Machiavelli asks, what would have happened if Julius were pope at a time when caution was the dominant quality that a prince needed? Well, I doubt if he would have been successful. I doubt if he could have changed his stripes, if you will. So Machiavelli is saying that certain princes are going to be successful or not if their style, if their personality, if their character matches the needs of the time, but the very greatest princes—rare quality—the very greatest princes can adapt and can succeed whatever the situation.

We've had these discussions in our own country about various American presidents. Do we have the right president at the right time? You take a president who was in office during a time when there was a lot of prosperity and you say, could this person have rescued us if we were in a time of economic despair? Or, somebody who had a program for success and progress within the states, would that person have been a good wartime president? And, we raise the question do we have a system of government where, in fact, it is likely we're going to get the kinds of leaders we need at a particular time? An interesting question—it's an interesting ongoing question. Machiavelli, again, gets us to think about that question. It's not just is this person smarter than that person, is this person more skilled than that person, but it's much more, does this person have the right set of skills and temperament and whatever to preside at this particular time, given the needs of the country and its situation, not just internally but in the world?

So, after this discussion of fortune, Machiavelli turns to his final piece in *The Prince*—not really another topic, but an exhortation. It's an exhortation to drive the barbarians—barbarians means foreigners—out of Italy. Let's review; Italy, I know you all know by now, was invaded by the French and then later on other foreigners, beginning in 1494. This was a great tragedy to Machiavelli because it broke up that 40-year sort of fairly peaceful balance of power that had been set up in 1454 by Cosimo de' Medici and others. But, as Machiavelli looks around, he says, perhaps, now is the time to get rid of the barbarians and to begin that process of reordering and restructuring and restabilizing Italian society. We think that, probably, Machiavelli might have thought that Cesare Borgia would have been that guy, that liberator of Italy, but we know Cesare Borgia ultimately failed and of course died.

But now Machiavelli looks around in 1513, the year he writes *The Prince*, and he says, okay, of those five traditional great powers in Italy, two of them were run by the same family, the Medici in Florence and the Papacy where Leo X, a member of the Medici family, was elected pope in 1513. And they, because they are of the same family, can work together to begin the process of Italy's liberation. He believes, Machiavelli does, there are already signs that this is going to happen and they're not just the signs of a political hardhead. He sees, what we would call, prophetic actions in nature even, that indicate the Medici are going to succeed. This really surprises us. We don't expect Machiavelli to interpret a lightening bolt or a flood or any kind of a natural phenomenon as a prophetic act that will tell us something about God's plans. It reminds us that as modern as Machiavelli sounds to us, Machiavelli is also a guy who shares many of the beliefs and values of his own time. But, Machiavelli believes that similar to the parting of the Red Sea at the time of the Exodus, there are signs in the world in which he lives that suggest that the Medici are the ones to liberate Italy from the barbarians. What the Medici need to do, therefore, is to create an army of their own citizens and not an army of mercenaries or of auxiliaries and they can be successful. He says the Spanish, who seem invincible, in fact cannot withstand cavalry and the Swiss infantry, the great mercenary bodies of Swiss; they, too, are not invincible.

Machiavelli ends with a great patriotic exhortation. Let's take a look at the very end of *The Prince*:

> This opportunity, therefore, must not be allowed to pass by so that Italy may behold her redeemer after so long a time, nor can I express with what love he will be received in all those territories that have suffered through these foreign floods. What with their thirst for revenge, what with stubborn loyalty, what with devotion, with what tears, what doors will be closed

to him? What people will deny him their obedience? What envy could oppose him? What Italian could deny him homage? This barbarian dominion stinks and everyone's nostrils therefore may your illustrious house [the Medici] take up this task with the spirit and hope with which just enterprises are begun so that under your banner this country may be ennobled and under your auspices these words of Petrarch may come true.

Here's the quote from Petrarch: "Virtue will seize arms against frenzy and the battle will be brief, for ancient valor is not yet dead in Italian hearts." We know that Machiavelli is this great careful-thinking hardheaded politician, and he is all that, and we respect him; we even admire him for it. But it's interesting to see, at the end, Machiavelli also has a dream, a dream of an Italy that is safe, secure, with a prince who is respected and honored and feared and obeyed. Machiavelli is also Machiavelli the dreamer.

Lecture Twelve
Livy, the Roman Republic, and Machiavelli

Scope:

Although we have examined the influence of Humanist thought and ancient history on Machiavelli, it is necessary to return to this theme more precisely as we turn to his most carefully thought-out and longest book on political thought, *The Discourses on the First Ten Books of Livy.*

In order for us to understand what Machiavelli is doing and why he so honors the Roman Republic, we will need to step back a bit and describe that period of history, as well as provide a broad view of how Livy understood Rome's republican past.

I will then examine the extent to which Machiavelli's *Discourses* is a commentary on ancient history and whether his reading of Livy is primarily an entrée into the world of Florentine and Italian politics during Machiavelli's own lifetime.

Outline

I. We now turn to Machiavelli's *Discourses on the First Ten Books of Livy.*

    A. Machiavelli's *Discourses* is his most thoughtful and considered work.

    B. The length of this work, however, plus the fact that it is a series of discourses on a book that very few people read today, means that often, readers do not get the full impact of what Machiavelli has to say.

II. Livy was a historian who lived from about 64 B.C. to A.D. 17.

    A. Livy was read during the Middle Ages, and Dante praises him as "the poet who does not err."

    B. In the Renaissance, Livy was seen as particularly important to republican Florence because he wrote the most complete history of Rome's republican period.

    C. He was from what is now the city of Padua in the north of Italy.

D. After writing the history of early Rome, he came to Rome and became an acquaintance of the Emperor Augustus.

E. He never held office.

F. Based on mistakes he makes about military matters, historians have concluded that Livy was never a soldier.

III. Livy wrote 142 books (more accurately scrolls) of the history of Rome, beginning with its legendary foundations.

    A. Of the 142 books, only 35 still exist.

    B. In today's terms, Livy's history was about 9,000 modern pages long.

    C. We have brief summaries of the missing books, with a couple of exceptions.

    D. From the amount of writing Livy did, we can conclude that he did not do independent historical research but relied on earlier histories of Rome.

IV. What survives of Livy's works are two major pieces of his original.

    A. The first surviving section, which is what Machiavelli writes about, consists of the first 10 books.

        1. Book I is the largely legendary history of Rome from its founding in about 753 B.C. until the end of the kings and the establishment of the republic (traditionally dated 509 B.C.).

        2. Books II–V carry the story from the republic's beginnings to the capture of Rome by the Gauls (traditionally 390 B.C.).

        3. The next five books tell the story of Rome's conquest of Italy, ending about 293 B.C. (Note: The territory comprising the modern nation of Italy did not all come under Roman rule until several centuries later.)

    B. The other piece of Livy's history that survives begins with the Second Punic War (against Hannibal) and continues through Rome's conquest of much of the Greek-speaking world.

V. The first 10 books, especially the first five, contain most of the best-known stories of the ancient Roman Republic.

    A. Romulus founds Rome and kills his brother Remus.

B. The first Brutus puts an end to the Roman monarchy when he kills Tarquin the Proud.

C. Heroic Roman tales are included in Livy's early history, such as those of Cincinnatus, the Roman farmer being called to leave his plow and go out and lead Rome to victory, and Horatius, standing by himself to defend a bridge until it could be destroyed and Rome saved from the Etruscans.

VI. Livy has often been criticized in modern times for his history.

A. Because he does not do what we would call archival research, even when that was possible, modern historians tend to see him as unoriginal.

B. The city of Rome itself is really the hero of his history, and there is a sense that its success was providential.

C. In tune with the times and with earlier Roman historians, such as Sallust, Livy is a moralist who sees history as a way to present virtue and vice and their consequences.

VII. Machiavelli clearly loved not only Livy's writing but also the story that Livy tells, for the Roman Republic lasted about 500 years and grew from a small town to the dominant force in the Mediterranean during the republican period.

A. In *The Prince*, Machiavelli shows his knowledge of and interest in the early history of Rome.

B. Like Livy, Machiavelli is not so much rummaging around the past for its own sake, but he is interested in drawing contemporary lessons.

C. Machiavelli makes use of many examples from his own time, as well as from all of classical antiquity in the *Discourses*.

VIII. Before looking at the *Discourses*, in which Machiavelli makes clear his republican sympathies, it is worthwhile remembering the classical definition of a republic.

A. This definition is rooted in Aristotle's thought but received its classic form in the writing of a 2nd-century-B.C. Greek historian, Polybius, writing in Rome.

B. A republic is a mixed constitution, consisting of elements of monarchy, aristocracy, and democracy.

C. One of the greatest advantages of this mixed form of government was stability, something Machiavelli longed for in his turbulent Florence and Italy.

Recommended Readings:

Julia Bondanella and Peter Bondanella, "Introduction," in Machiavelli's *Discourses on Livy*, translated by Julia Bondanella and Peter Bondanella, pp. vii–xxii.

T. J. Luce, "Introduction," in Livy's *The Rise of Rome* (Books I–V), translated by T. J. Luce, pp. ix–xxvii.

Article by Quentin Skinner, in *Machiavelli and Republicanism*, Gisela Bock, Quentin Skinner, and Maurizio Viroli, et al., eds., pp. 121–141.

Questions to Consider:

1. Who is Livy and why did his writings matter so much to Machiavelli?

2. What are the stories that you know from the early Roman Republic? Romulus and Remus? The rape of Lucretia and the establishment of the republic? Cincinnatus at the plow? Horatius at the bridge?

3. Recognizing that the commonly heard "a republic is a representative democracy" is an insufficient definition, how should we think of *republic* when reading Livy and Machiavelli?

Lecture Twelve—Transcript
Livy, the Roman Republic, and Machiavelli

Okay, now this course is going to get good. We have finished our discussion of the most famous of Machiavelli's works, *The Prince*, a work that I assume all of you know something about. I'm sure many of you have read it probably in its entirety. Perhaps in a Western Civilization course, or History course, of Political Science course, you've certainly read snippets of it. It's well known, oft quoted, oft misquoted, often understood, often misunderstood. But, what I want to argue is that Machiavelli's most thoughtful and most profound work, and a work that's had a great deal of influence although not to the extent of *The Prince*, is his *Discourses on the First Ten Books of Livy*. We're going to spend this lecture learning a little bit about Livy and the Roman Republic, and then the seven following lectures will be discussing this important book of Machiavelli's. My goal is to persuade you even if you have not heard of, and almost certainly not read all of *The Discourses*, to go out and get it. And, to spend some time with it and to ruminate on it and I think you will find it will repay the time that you invest in reading this very thoughtful, carefully conceived book by Niccolò Machiavelli.

If I'm right, if it is such a good book, why doesn't everybody read it? Why is it a kind of secret, if you will, from many people who know the name Machiavelli or have read something of Machiavelli? Let me suggest two, I think, fairly obvious reasons. Number one, it's pretty long, much longer—three, four, five times longer even—than *The Prince*. Of course, what that means is that—let's be practical about this—most people who read Machiavelli, read Machiavelli in college and if you're going to read a work of Machiavelli's, you're going to read the most famous one and one that's short because there is some advantage of teaching a whole work rather than little snippets. And so, the very length of *The Discourses* that Machiavelli wrote work against it being nearly as well known as *The Prince*.

Secondly, it is a series of discourses—three long discourses subdivided each into many chapters on the first ten books of Livy. Wherever you are, in your car or in your living room, put up your hand if you've read the first ten books of Livy. I'm just imagining now, but I don't think I see very many hands. This is the first five books of Livy, so multiply by two and you see that Livy's first ten books, which tell the story from the founding of Rome until the year

293 B.C., or B.C.E.—depending on how you date things—those first ten books are very long. They have a lot of names. It's a chronological approach to early Roman history and even if you took a course in Roman history in college, it's unlikely that you read more than a small snippet of Livy, if you read any at all. Livy is one of those authors, sort of like Cicero, who in the 20th century probably began to have a reputation that declined. Actually, his began to decline in the 18th century, rightly or wrongly. And so, therefore, *The Discourses* is hard to read if you don't know what Machiavelli is discoursing on. And so, those two things, the length and the fact that he's writing based on Livy, conspire together, if you will, although unconsciously, to keep many people from tackling this most important work of Machiavelli.

Let's turn for most of this lecture to a look at Livy, and get to know Livy and the subject of Livy's history of Rome. First of all, Livy, of course, wrote in Latin; he was a Roman, lived at the time of Augustus. In fact, to be precise, he was born in 64, we think, B.C. and he died in 17 A.D. So, he lived through the reign of the Emperor Augustus as the republic was coming to an end. Okay, that's who Livy was. But because Livy wrote in Latin, his writings, those that have been preserved—I'll explain in a minute that not all of Livy's history survives—but those parts that we have today, of course, were copied during the Middle Ages and read some. Not a lot, but some. Livy was not unknown. Dante, in fact, pays Livy a high compliment, writing just after 1300. He refers to Livy as "that historian who does not err, who does not make mistakes." But during the Renaissance, Livy became the historian for the Humanists in Florence. Because, as we saw, one of the important parts of the Humanist movement was: We go back and learn about the ancient past and it becomes a way of us understanding ourselves and living better. Well, I've already set up this equation, but let remind you, Rome was a republic. Florence is a republic in Machiavelli's time, as he serves the republican government of Florence, and even during the eras of Medici rule, the propaganda always was that the first Medici are first citizens and it really is a republic still, even though the Medici were in charge. So, you've got a republic in Rome written about primarily by Livy and you've got this republic Florence. Of course, Livy has something to say to that society and so Livy became enormously popular.

As I pointed out, Machiavelli had in his home as a boy a copy of Livy—a printed copy, not a manuscript copy—that his father obtained by doing the index. He was paid for doing the index by getting a copy of the book. Again, early printed books were still quite expensive; it wasn't until early in the 16th century, and probably more in Germany than in Italy, that the value of the printing press as a way of widely distributing materials to people who could have never afforded hand-copied books was understood. So, we have this great popularity of Livy during the Renaissance.

Livy came from what's now called the city of Padua, or Padova in Italian, in the northern part of Italy. He did a lot of his writing while living in Padua and then came to Rome and caught the attention of, and became an acquaintance of, the Emperor Augustus; however, he was never part of Augustus's inner circle. He was never one of Augustus's major advisors; he didn't write on commission from Augustus. In fact, it's interesting he apparently never held any office at all, something we might expect him to have done. Furthermore, although we know almost nothing about his life other than what we can glean from what he wrote about Roman history, it appears he was never a soldier because as military historians have pointed out, he makes a lot of mistakes when describing military matters and so people assume he did not have much experience as a soldier. Livy wrote 142, what are then called, books—more accurately, scrolls—of Roman history, 142 of them. Beginning with the foundation of Rome—that is to say, all that Romulus and Remus stuff; we'll talk about it and Machiavelli will talk about it, indeed.

Of those 142 books of history that he wrote, only 35 still exist. Most of Livy is gone. Is there any hope we'll someday find it? Not much. It was gone, obviously, already in Machiavelli's time. We don't think there are any manuscripts that we're likely to discover in a musty old library somewhere that, alas, have all of Livy's history. If we were to take all 142 books of Livy's history and print it in modern editions like the first five books here, Livy wrote about 9,000 modern pages of Roman history. I want you to think about that—9,000 pages. Now, if we think about an average book size today as being 300 pages, okay, I want you to think about how many books Livy wrote. It was an enormous undertaking. We do know what was in the missing book with a couple exceptions because later writers did write summaries of each of the books of Livy. We can conclude simply from the amount of stuff. Again, this is five books, he wrote 142 books; imagine, if you will, that you've got one of these volumes that's, say, ¾ of an inch in front of you, containing the first five books and then multiply that, remember he wrote 142 books, and you know that Livy was a shelf of Roman history in modern print.

We don't think, however, that Livy did what we call archival research; he could have. There were a lot of documents, there were a lot of lists that survived in ancient Rome, not all the way back to the time of the Romulus and Remus, but back several hundred years. There's no reason to think from what Livy tells us in his history that, in fact, Livy did any of that sort of research at all. What he seems to have done is rely on the writing of earlier Roman historians, so that almost all of what he writes until he gets close to his own time, is filtered through earlier historians and probably still contains a good deal of oral tradition, some of which had been written and some of which was still in oral form. So, we don't think of Livy as a researcher; we think of him as a writer of history. Now, that sounds odd to us today because, especially for academic historians like myself, it seems that the two—researcher and historian—go hand in hand. And, in fact, it's very easy for modern historians for not doing what we would have done, or what we think we would have done, had we lived in his era knowing that there were documents to look at. But, we need to remember who Livy was and who Livy wasn't.

Now, of these 142 books, one of the interesting questions is, what survives? Which 35 books of the 142 survive? What do they cover? Let me suggest there are two big chunks, a very early chunk and then a chunk that begins in the 3rd century and goes into the 2nd century. I'm going to go over both of these in more detail, the first more than the second because the first is the part from which Machiavelli draws his examples in his *Discourses*. Let's look at those first ten books. Book 1 is the legendary beginning of Rome, again Romulus and Remus, and tells a story of the traditional founding date of Rome, which was 753 B.C.; those things cannot be confirmed, at least at that level of specificity, by historians today. And, book 1 carries the story down to 509, the traditional date of the founding of the Roman Republic. The great event that founds the Roman Republic is that a guy named Brutus—obviously, this is almost 500 years before the more famous Brutus—but Brutus carries out the expulsion of the last of the Roman kings and, therefore, that's the date that marks the founding of the republic. So book 1 covers this period from the founding through the kings to the establishment of the republic.

Books 2–5 carry that story down through the year 390 B.C., when Rome is besieged by and briefly taken by a tribe from the north called the Gauls. This was an important dividing line in Roman history. By the way, it remains so for a long time because it was the last time that the city of Rome was actually taken. Hannibal might have been able to, but he didn't, so it was the last time Rome was taken in 800 years. The next time is 410 A.D., when the Goths come and for several days sack the city of Rome. We need to understand that's why people in 410 A.D. were so shocked, because it hadn't been done in 800 years; it hadn't been done since 390. So, books 1–5 start with the founding of Rome by Romulus and go down to the year 390.

Then, the next five books, so that we remember that this the discourses on the first ten books of Livy, books 6–10 carry the story to the year 293 B.C. They are largely the story, those 6–10, largely the story of Rome's beginning to expand in Italy. Sometimes we refer to these books as the conquest of Italy, but we need to remember that it was really the conquest of much of central Italy. For example, Sicily didn't come under Roman domination for a long time and the area up now where Milan is and the foothills of the Alps and so on, that didn't come into Roman control until several centuries later. So, we're looking at though the first expansion. Rome was essentially a town on the Tiber that didn't control much beyond what we think of as the city of Rome today. By 293, it had conquered a fair chunk of Italy. So, these are the stories, the stories from Romulus and Remus down to 293 that Machiavelli will somewhat systematically retell, draw lessons from, and make comparisons with to modern events in *The Discourses*. Therefore, if you want to do some preliminary reading for Machiavelli's *Discourses*, assignment A is to go read the first ten books of Livy. If you don't have time to do that, at least read some sort of organized narrative summary of Roman history for that period so you know what it is that Machiavelli is drawing from. That would be a very useful thing to do.

Now, beginning after book 10, there's a gap. The next books are lost and we get the second chunk of Livy. I simply want to point this out fairly briefly, beginning with the Punic Wars, the war between Rome and Carthage. All the stories you know, probably, of Hannibal crossing the Alps, and all that stuff with elephants, and all those Hannibal stories are preserved for us by Livy. Again, he got them out of older histories, but those older histories, by and large, don't survive. And so, therefore, we rely on Livy for this great story of the struggle between Rome and Carthage and the next chunk of Livy that starts with the Punic Wars that continues to about the year 150, by which time Rome has conquered parts of North Africa and much of the Greek-speaking world. And then, the more modern history of the Roman Republic from 146 or so on—all of that's gone. We don't have any of that from Livy, although we have other sources for it, of course. So, you'll notice that although *The Discourses* are based on the first ten books of Livy, you can tell from the extended example he gives of Hannibal in *The Prince* that Machiavelli knows the rest of Livy and not just these ten books.

Now, the first ten books contain most of the stories that you probably know about early Roman history. First of all, of course, they contain, as I said, the story of Romulus and Remus. That's always good; I mean, that comes with she-wolf, that comes with brother murdering brother, Romulus kills Remus, and by the way, Machiavelli's going to have a lot to say about whether that was an okay thing to do. That's an interesting question in and of itself. The first ten books, as I said, contain the story of Brutus expelling the last king Tarquin the Proud and, therefore, ushering in the establishment of the republic. And then, there are all those good heroic tales of good old virtuous Roman Republicans, some of which you might know. Horatius standing by himself to defend a bridge until it could be destroyed so that Rome could not be conquered. And, there's the famous story of Cincinnatus being called to leave his plow and go out and lead Rome to victory. Those are also stories in the first ten books of Livy, stories again that Machiavelli will comment on. The Cincinnatus story, of course, is very important even in American history. After all, if you look at the statue of 1775 of the Minutemen at Lexington and Concorde, what do you discover? They are men leaving their plow—well, of course, they weren't literally leaving their plow—but also it identifies them with that virtue and that citizen-soldier notion of the ancient Roman republic. It is no accident that George Washington named the veterans' organization at the end of the American Revolution the Order of the Cincinnati, which is simply plural of Cincinnatus. We're a nation of Cincinnatuses, if you will, those are the guys that won the freedom of the states from Britain. And so, those are stories that are passed down directly or indirectly to us; they are all found in their oldest form that survives in Livy.

Now, let me suggest, I've already mentioned this, that modern historical writers have not been all that kind to Livy. I pointed out one reason. Livy could have done some archival research, although it's doubtful he could have written 143 scrolls if he'd done so; he could have done archival research, but he didn't and you can imagine academic historians tend to sort of shudder a bit at that. Secondly, if we were asked, who is the hero of Livy's history of the Roman Republic, the answer is Rome is the hero and providentially so. It just seems to have been in the cards that Rome was going to succeed and that's a kind of interpretation that modern historians are uncomfortable with. We don't tend to write about things happening providentially. Furthermore, very much in tune with the historiographical traditions of his own time, Livy was unapologetic in trying to say here are good guys and bad guys, here are lessons to imitate, and here are lessons to run away from. He is a moralist and he believes that, in many ways, the value of history is teaching right and wrong. It's a very moral approach to history. What do we learn from history? We learn how to act well and what the consequences are, how to act badly and what the consequences are. By the way, although I think we can say, in general, Machiavelli agrees with the notion that what we want to do is draw some very practical lessons from the past, not just treat it for its own sake, nevertheless, Machiavelli will not be afraid to criticize Livy as wrong or naïve. His respect for Livy is great; that does not mean, certainly, that Livy is infallible.

By the way, I just want to point out, parenthetically, that this notion of history as a moral undertaking is very important and was up until the 19th century when a kind of science or social science model of history was created, first by the Germans and then later on it came to the United States and the rest of the world. And, if you read other early Roman historians—by the way, I particularly recommend the Roman historian Sallust who wrote two short works that are very interesting—you will see that, once again, they are openly, obviously, and directly designed to be part of the literature of morality. They are about how people should act and what happens when people act badly.

Why was Machiavelli so attracted to Livy and his history of the Roman republic? Well, again, Machiavelli's a Florentine living in a republic and I've already talked about that in general, but let me suggest something that's a bit more specific. If we look at the Roman republic, here is a way to describe it; it lasted a very long time. If we just use the traditional dates and historians can fiddle with them on either end—and rightfully so, that's an okay thing for historians to do, we do a lot of fiddling—you begin in 509 B.C. and usually give the date of the end of the republic as 27 B.C. when Augustus sort of declares himself as, well, Augustus; it's a title, after all, not a name. 509 to 27—you'd have to be a wizard to know it's about 500 years. The republic lasted a long time. It didn't last forever, but it lasted a very long time and that in itself says you must be doing something right. Secondly, when the republic began, it was a dot on the map. It was what we would call the town or city of Rome and not much else. By the time the republic ended, it controlled virtually the entire Mediterranean, some of what we would call the Middle East, all of what we would call Spain and France or Gaul; it was very big, very wealthy, and very powerful. You've got to respect that. Again, you've got to say, they did something right for a very long time.

If you simply gauge the Roman Republic by its success, its stability, and its growth, you've got to say, by gum, there are going to be some lessons here that we can learn from those folks way back then. And so, we can understand why Machiavelli not just as someone who was given a Humanist education, or someone whose dad happened to have a copy of Livy, but if we remember the subject matter of Livy's history, we can see why Machiavelli was so impressed and we need to remember that, therefore, Machiavelli respects Livy as a historian and is extraordinarily interested in the subject of Livy's history. You know, sometimes it's one and sometimes it's the other. I've had students say to me, "I take courses, but I'm not very interested in what you teach. I just sort of enjoy you're lectures" or whatever it might be. By the way, that's not really as flattering as they think it is. I want them to love the stuff I teach. They like the historian; they don't like the subject matter. Other times you find the students like the subject matter, but they don't like your approach to it. I'll teach a course on the Middle Ages and students will be disappointed because I don't teach them how to make chain mail or how to build a catapult. And, therefore, they're interested in the subject matter of the Middle Ages, but they're not interested in what I have to say about it.

Well, Machiavelli was interested in Livy as a writer and thinker and also the subject of Livy's great book—that is to say, the ancient Roman Republic. Machiavelli admired the fact that Livy was not, what we might call today, an antiquarian. He was not really writing history for its own sake, but for what it can teach us about how we should behave, how we should act, and how we can understand the world we live in today better. History was a guide, sometimes a warning for us today, not simply an obscure intellectual enterprise.

Machiavelli enriches Livy because even though this book we're going to be looking at is indeed based on the first ten books of Livy, Machiavelli, as he did in *The Prince*, throws in lots of contemporary examples. He'll draw some point from Livy and say, the best example of that, and then he'll tell something that happened three days ago. He does, in one case, by the way, literally do that; he says here's something that happened just a few days ago. It helps us date when he wrote *The Discourses* so Machiavelli is going to continue that process of not simply reporting about the ancient past, but also giving modern analogs, modern illustrations of points that Livy makes when he finds those to be the most useful.

Now, this is a book that exposes Machiavelli as a—obviously small "r," I won't keep saying that—a small "r" republican. You might not get that; some readers today say, you know I can sort of see that in *The Prince*. It isn't right there in the open, he isn't saying it out loud, but I sort of get that. Maybe so, maybe if we only had *The Prince* there would be those who would read and say, you know this guy's really a republican at heart, but probably not many. But, Machiavelli is openly, clearly, someone who prefers republican government; there's no secret about that as we read *The Discourses*. Therefore, I want to end this introductory lecture by saying, what does Machiavelli mean by the word republic? We use it a lot. We take a Pledge of Allegiance to the flag and to the republic for which it stands. We use that word a great deal. I ask students very often, give me a quick definition of republic and their answer very often is, a republic is a representative democracy. Bag that one. That will not do. That's not what Machiavelli means at all. Beginning with Aristotle, a definition of a republic emerges in the ancient world, and it's one that Machiavelli's going to use.

It takes its clearest form not from Aristotle, but from a 2nd-century— listen to this—2nd-century B.C. Greek historian writing in the Greek language, but writing in Rome about Roman history, named Polybius. This is basically how Aristotle and even more so Polybius understand a republic. Okay, you can be governed in three ways; you can be governed by one, you can be governed by few, or you can be governed by many. We might today say monarchy, aristocracy, or democracy. The problem is that none of those is very stable, that monarchy can turn into tyranny, aristocracy can turn into something like oligarchy government by the wealthy rather than government by the best—which is what aristocracy, after all, means in its original

Greek—and democracy can turn into mob rule. So, all of these are fairly unstable forms of government. A republic is a mixed constitution. It has elements of monarchy, elements of aristocracy, and elements of a democracy and using a combination of those three basic forms—government by one, government by few, and government by many—a good republic is stable. By the way, think how important that is to Machiavelli. He lost his job in Florence when the government changed from being a true republic, he believed, to the Medici coming in and ruling. Think of all the general instability in Italy; what you need is something that lasts, something that's stable, something that is strong enough institutionally and conceptually to survive all the inevitable challenges and changes of fortune or human action that take place. And so, Machiavelli comes to look at Rome as a republic. He sees its constitution, he sees its longevity, and he sees its successes and, therefore, it really is the most appropriate and useful thing that Machiavelli can study and present to those whom he hopes will liberate Italy and restore Italy to peace and stability.

Timeline

1507	Machiavelli named as chancellor of a group of officials charged with raising a militia in Florence.
1512	The Medici return as rulers of Florence; Machiavelli is dismissed from his offices.
1513	Machiavelli is arrested and tortured but soon receives a pardon and moves to his family's estate at Sant' Andrea in Percussina. He writes *The Prince*.
1513–1517	Machiavelli writes the *Discourses* and, while doing so, also composes *The Art of War*.
1518–1519	Machiavelli writes his first and best-known play, *The Mandrake Root*.
1520	Machiavelli completes his life of Castruccio Castracani and is commissioned by Giulio de'Medici to write a history of Florence.
1521	Publication of Machiavelli's *Art of War*.
1526	Machiavelli finishes his *Florentine Histories*.
1527	Medici expelled from Florence. Machiavelli dies.
1531	Publication of Machiavelli's *Discourses*.
1532	Publication of Machiavelli's *The Prince*.
1559	Machiavelli's books placed on the Index of Prohibited Books.
1640	First English translation of *The Prince* published.

Glossary

Art of War: The only political work of Machiavelli published during his lifetime.

Auxiliaries: Foreign troops borrowed from an ally. Machiavelli believed that auxiliaries were worthless.

Ciompi Rebellion: An uprising by workers in the woolen industry in Florence in 1378. Despite temporary success, the rebellion was thoroughly put down by 1381.

Council of Florence: An ecumenical council of the Roman Church meeting in 1439 that temporarily patched the split between the Roman and Orthodox Churches.

Decemvirs: A group of 10 men appointed in the early Roman Republic to create laws.

Dictator: An occasional office in the Roman Republic. A dictator would be elected for a short period of time to supersede the regularly elected officials in matters of war. Cincinnatus and Fabius Maximus were famous dictators.

Florence: An independent city-state located in Tuscany. It had at least the façade of a republican government during the late Middle Ages and into the 15th century. From 1434 to 1494, the Medici family ruled. Florence returned to a republican form of government in 1494, but the Medici returned to power in 1512. After a brief republican government beginning in 1527, the Medici became hereditary rulers and eventually grand dukes of Tuscany.

Florentine Republic: Could refer to the government of Florence before 1434 but usually refers to the government of Florence between 1494 and 1512. Machiavelli was an official of the Florentine Republic from 1498 until its fall in 1512.

Fortuna: An Italian word often translated as "Fortune." In the classical world, Fortune was said to be a woman and could, to some extent, be controlled or her effects influenced. In the Christianization of the concept of Fortune in the Middle Ages, the concept came to be associated with fate and was considered totally out of human control. Machiavelli returns to a more classical definition of Fortune, feeling that some things are out of our control but maintaining that we can be prepared for Fortune and her effects.

Guelfs and Ghibellines: Two political factions present in Italian cities in the later Middle Ages. The Guelfs generally favored papal power, while the Ghibellines supported the Holy Roman Emperor. Florence was a predominantly Guelf city, although there were two short periods of Ghibelline rule in the 13th century. Around 1300, the Guelfs split into White and Black factions, so named because a woman in one of the factions was named Bianca, "white" in Italian.

Humanism: The dominant educational program in Renaissance Florence. Humanists studied the classics and modeled their thought and writings on exemplars from classical antiquity.

Lucca: City in Tuscany that retained its independence from Florence. Home of Castruccio Castracani.

Machiavellian, Machiavel: Adjectives created within a century of Machiavelli's death, usually meaning someone who is ruthless and will use any means to achieve his ends.

(*La*) *Mandragola* (*Mandrake Root*): Machiavelli's most famous play.

Mercenaries: Foreign hired troops, usually a body of men with a commander (*condottiere*). Machiavelli thought they were worthless.

Mixed constitution: A form of government consisting of elements of monarchy, aristocracy, and democracy.

Pazzi conspiracy: An unsuccessful plot to put an end to Medici rule in Florence in 1478. Lorenzo de'Medici escaped, although his brother Giuliano was killed.

Pisa: City in Tuscany that was a traditional enemy of Florence. Florence captured the city in 1408 but had difficulty controlling it.

Pistoia: A Tuscan city near Florence that was part of the Florentine city-state but was often difficult for Florence to control.

Renaissance: Term used to describe cultural, intellectual, and artistic changes beginning in Italy in the 14th century and centered in Florence in the 15th century. Refers specifically to the revival of, interest in, and imitation of Greek and Roman classics.

Republic: A form of government defined as a mixed government with elements of monarchy, aristocracy, and democracy. Florence prided itself on its republican heritage, although it only roughly approximated the classic definition of a republic.

Risorgimento: The movement in the 19th century that led to the unification of Italy. Machiavelli was regarded as a "prophet" of Italian unity by leaders of the Risorgimento.

Romagna: An area of north central Italy that came under the rule of Cesare Borgia.

Sant' Andrea in Percussina: Village about 11 kilometers south of Florence. It was here that Machiavelli lived after leaving Florence in 1513. While in Sant' Andrea, he wrote *The Prince* and his *Discourses on Livy*.

Siena: Independent republic south of Florence and a traditional rival of Florence.

Venice: A republic in the northeastern part of the Italian peninsula. It was often regarded as a model for a republic because of its success and longevity. Machiavelli was not as enthusiastic about Venice as a model as many of his fellow Florentines were.

Virtù: An Italian word often translated as "virtue" but whose meaning is not exactly what modern people mean when they use the word. It suggests strong and manly action (*vir* = man in Latin) and does not necessarily connote "ethical."

Biographical Notes

Alexander VI (1431–1503): A pope whose name was Rodrigo Borgia. He spent much of his reign establishing a territory for his son Cesare and finding a husband for his daughter Lucrezia.

Aristotle (384–322 B.C.): Greek philosopher who wrote a great deal about politics and the idea of a mixed constitution.

Borgia, Cesare (1475–1507): Son of Pope Alexander VI. He ruled much of the Romagna but fell from power when his father died and Julius II became pope. He was something of a hero for Machiavelli.

Brutus (fl. 510 B.C.): The Roman most responsible for the expulsion of the last king and the establishment of the republic in 509 B.C. The Brutus who assassinated Julius Caesar in 44 B.C. claimed to be the direct descendant of this Brutus.

Castracani, Castruccio (1281–1328): Military leader from Lucca. Machiavelli wrote a biography of him as a prelude to writing his *Florentine Histories*.

Cicero, Marcus Tullius (106–43 B.C.): Statesman, orator, and writer in the late Roman Republic. In his famous book *On Duties* (*De officiis*), he outlines the qualities of a good leader. Machiavelli challenges his widely held beliefs.

Clement VII (1478–1534): Born Giulio de'Medici, son of Giuliano de'Medici, who was killed in 1478 during the Pazzi conspiracy. Elected pope in 1523. He commissioned Machiavelli's *Florentine Histories*.

Fabius Maximus (d. 203 B.C.): Elected dictator of Rome after Hannibal defeated Rome in the battle of Cannae in 216 B.C.E. He was famous for his plan not to attack Hannibal directly; thus, he is sometimes known as Fabius the Delayer.

Gracchi: Refers to the brothers Tiberius (d. 133 B.C.) and Gaius (d. 121 B.C.) Gracchus, both of whom sought to establish agrarian laws calling for major land reform in the second half of the 2nd century B.C.E.

Hannibal (247–182 B.C.): The Carthaginian general who conducted the Second Punic War against Rome.

Harrington, James (1611–1677): Most important English political writer to incorporate elements of Machiavelli's republican philosophy into his and, hence, into English political thought. His principal work is called *Oceana*.

Julius II (1443–1513): The pope who succeeded, after the very brief reign of Pius III, Alexander VI. Julius was quite a military figure; he commissioned Michelangelo to paint the ceiling of the Sistine Chapel.

Leo X (1475–1521): Elected pope in 1513. He was born Giovanni de'Medici, the son of Lorenzo de'Medici. Machiavelli held out great hope that having the papacy and Florence ruled by the same family would lead to the expulsion of foreign armies from Italy.

Livy (c. 64 B.C.–A.D. 17): His complete name was Titus Livius. Livy wrote a long history of Rome, only parts of which survive. The first 10 books deal with the history of the Roman Republic before about 386 B.C. Machiavelli's *Discourses* are an extended commentary on those 10 books.

Machiavelli, Niccolò (1469–1527): Florentine official and author. Author of *The Prince*, *Discourses on Livy*, *Florentine Histories*, and other works.

Medici: Florentine family that dominated political matters there after 1434. The Medici were expelled in 1494, returned in 1512, expelled again in 1527, and permanently returned in 1530. They ruled Florence during most of the Renaissance.

Medici, Cosimo de' (1389–1464): De facto ruler of Florence from 1434–1464. He did not hold office but controlled who did. He was much venerated and known as the "father" of his country.

Medici, Giuliano de' (1453–1478): Brother of Lorenzo de'Medici who was assassinated in 1478 during the Pazzi conspiracy. He was also the father of Pope Clement VII.

Medici, Lorenzo de' (1449–1492): Grandson of Cosimo and ruler of Florence from 1469–1492. He escaped an assassination attempt during the Pazzi conspiracy of 1478. Lorenzo was known as a great patron of the arts and is often referred to as "the Magnificent." His son Giovanni became Pope Leo X.

Numa Pompilius: According to legend, succeeded Romulus as king of Rome and established religious customs.

Polybius (c. 200–c. 118 B.C.): A Greek who wrote an important history of Rome. He best articulated the idea of Rome as a republic having a mixed constitution.

Romulus: Legendary founder of Rome in the 8th century B.C.

Savonarola, Girolamo (1452–1498): A Dominican friar born in Ferrara who became the most important political figure in Florence following the expulsion of the Medici in 1494. He claimed to be a prophet and tried to carry out a moral cleansing of Florence. Machiavelli famously referred to him as an "unarmed prophet." In 1498, Savonarola was executed in Florence.

Soderini, Piero (1452–1522): Held the chief office (Gonfaloniere of Justice) in the Florentine Republic from 1502 to 1512. Machiavelli worked in the government while Soderini was in charge. Though Machiavelli recognized Soderini's competence, he criticized him for being too passive.

Tarquin (the Proud): The last king of Rome, expelled in 509 B.C.

Vettori, Francesco (1474–1539): Friend and correspondent of Machiavelli. He was serving as Florence's ambassador to the papacy when Machiavelli was composing *The Prince* in 1513, and he is the recipient of the famous letter in which Machiavelli describes life in Sant' Andrea in Percussina.

Bibliography

Works of Niccolò Machiavelli:

The Art of War. Translated by Christopher Lynch. Chicago: University of Chicago Press, 2003. This volume is not only a translation but also contains a lengthy interpretative essay and a glossary.

Discourses on Livy. Translated by Julia Bondanella and Peter Bondanella. Oxford: Oxford University Press, 1997. This is a complete and readable translation of Machiavelli's greatest work. It contains a useful introduction plus a bibliography and notes. It is the translation used in this course.

Florentine Histories. Translated by Laura Banfield and Harvey Mansfield. Princeton: Princeton University Press, 1988. This volume is a complete translation and has a brief but helpful introduction. This is the translation used in this course.

Machiavelli and His Friends: Their Personal Correspondence. Edited and translated by James Atkinson and David Sices. DeKalb: Northern Illinois University Press, 1996. This is the only complete collection in English of Machiavelli's correspondence, and it gives an important window into his life and thought.

The Portable Machiavelli. Edited and translated by Peter Bondanella and Mark Musa. New York: Penguin, 1979. Here is a convenient anthology of Machiavelli's writings, including selections from the *Discourses*, *The History of Florence*, and *The Art of War*. It contains *The Prince* in its entirety plus several letters, including the famous one of 1513 to his friend Vettori, and one of Machiavelli's plays, *The Mandrake Root*.

The Prince. Translated by Peter Bondanella. Oxford: Oxford University Press, 2005. This is an outstanding and lively translation. The introduction is by the famous Machiavelli scholar Maurizio Viroli. There are almost countless translations of this classic. In this course, the Bondanella translation is used.

Works Useful to the Study of Niccolò Machiavelli:

Bock, Gisela, Quentin Skinner, and Maurizio Viroli, et al., eds. *Machiavelli and Republicanism.* New York: Cambridge University Press, 1990. This is a wonderful collection of essays by many of the leading authorities on Machiavelli, including Quentin Skinner, Nicolai Rubenstein, John Najemy, and Maurizio Viroli. Most of the essays are about Machiavelli and his works, but one section focuses on Machiavelli's influence in the 17th and 18th centuries.

Brucker, Gene. *The Civic World of Early Renaissance Florence*. Princeton: Princeton University Press, 1977. Brucker is perhaps the most distinguished historian of Renaissance Florence in the English-speaking world. This book is a history of Florence from 1378 to the beginning of Medici rule in 1434 and, thus, covers a period of history that Machiavelli treats with great interest in his *Florentine Histories*.

————. *Renaissance Florence*. Huntington, NY: Krieger, 1975, reprint with additional materials. This work is Brucker's general history of Florence during the Renaissance and carries the story to the end of the republic, shortly after Machiavelli's death.

Cicero. *On Obligations*. Translated by P. G. Walsh. Oxford: Oxford University Press, 2000. It is useful for students of Machiavelli to read this work because it was so influential in the political thought of the Renaissance. Machiavelli boldly rejected most of Cicero's arguments about the moral basis of rulership.

De Grazia, Sebastian. *Machiavelli in Hell*. Princeton: Princeton University Press, 1989. A distinctive and somewhat unconventional biography, it received a Pulitzer Prize for biography.

Fiore, Silvia Ruffo. *Niccolò Machiavelli: An Annotated Bibliography of Modern Criticism and Scholarship*. New York: Greenwood Press, 1990. This work covers a half century of Machiavelli scholarship.

Gilbert, Felix. *Machiavelli and Guicciardini: Politics and History in Sixteenth-Century Florence*. Princeton: Princeton University Press, 1963. This is a classic work of Renaissance history. It examines the two greatest Florentine writers of Florentine history.

Guicciardini, Francesco. *Dialogue on the Government of Florence*. Edited and translated by Alison Brown. Cambridge: Cambridge University Press, 1994. This work, written by Machiavelli's contemporary and fellow historian, dates from the 1520s but is cast as a debate about Florence's government following the expulsion of the Medici in 1494.

————. *The History of Florence*. Translated by Mario Domandi. New York: Harper, 1970. This is Guicciardini's account of Florence from the death of Cosimo de'Medici and includes history that Machiavelli wrote about and events that Machiavelli took part in as an official of the Florentine Republic.

Hale, J. R. *Machiavelli and Renaissance Italy*. London: English Universities Press, 1961. Hale's biography is fairly short and focuses on the historical context in which Machiavelli's works were created.

Hulliung, Mark. *Citizen Machiavelli*. Princeton: Princeton University Press, 1984. This work argues that Machiavelli took issue with Humanist thought.

Johnson, Paul. *The Renaissance: A Short History*. New York: Modern Library, 2000. Although focusing on art, this is an elegant though brief history of the Renaissance and provides a good context for the study of Machiavelli.

Kristeller, Paul. *Renaissance Thought*. Two volumes. New York: Harper and Row, 1961, 1965. Not easy reading, but these tomes are the best exploration of thought in Florence before and during the time of Machiavelli.

Levy, Michael. *Florence: A Portrait*. Cambridge, MA: Harvard University Press, 1996. With an excellent text and lavish illustrations, this is both a serious history of the city of Florence and almost a coffee-table book.

Livy. *The Early History of Rome*. Translated by Aubrey de Selincourt. New York: Penguin, revised edition, 2002. In order to read the *Discourses on Livy*, ideally, one should read Livy. This translation is of Books I–V.

————. *The Rise of Rome: Books 1–5*. Translated by T. J. Luce. Oxford: Oxford University Press, 1999. This is a somewhat newer translation of the first five books of Livy than the one listed above.

————. *Rome and Italy*. Translated by Betty Radice. New York: Penguin, 1982. This is a translation of Books VI–X of Livy.

Mansfield, Harvey. *Machiavelli's New Modes: A Study of the Discourses on Livy*. Chicago: University of Chicago Press, 1979. Here is an extraordinary book-by-book, passage-by-passage commentary on Machiavelli's most significant work.

————. *Machiavelli's Virtue*. Chicago: University of Chicago Press, 1996. This book is an interesting look at Machiavelli as a thinker. Mansfield is sympathetic to Machiavelli. There are two chapters devoted to Machiavelli's *Florentine Histories*, which Mansfield also translated (see above).

Martines, Lauro. *April Blood: Florence and the Plot Against the Medici*. Oxford: Oxford University Press, 2003. Martines has provided a fascinating account of the conspiracy against the Medici in 1478 that Machiavelli used as his major example of the dangers of conspiracies.

————. *Power and Imagination*. This is arguably the best one-volume look at Italy in the age of the Renaissance. It not only deals with political history but is also an astute introduction to Renaissance culture; its chapter on Humanism is the best brief treatment of the subject in English.

————. *The Social World of the Florentine Humanists, 1390–1460*. Princeton: Princeton University Press, 1963. This has become a standard work on early Humanism in Florence and contains sketches of the most important figures.

Masters, Roger. *Fortune Is a River: Leonardo da Vinci and Niccolò Machiavelli's Magnificent Dream to Change the Course of Florentine History*. New York: Free Press, 1998. This book is a somewhat fanciful but certainly imaginative look at a plan to divert the Arno River so that it no longer flowed through rival Pisa. The title is taken from Machiavelli's discussion of Fortune in *The Prince*.

Najemy, John. *Between Friends: Discourses of Power and Desire in the Machiavelli-Vettori Letters of 1513–1515*. Princeton: Princeton University Press, 1993. These letters, which can be read in English (see *Machiavelli and His Friends*, above), are well analyzed by Najemy and provide important insights on Machiavelli while he was writing *The Prince* and the *Discourses*.

Pocock, J. G. A. *The Machiavellian Moment: Florentine Political Thought and the Atlantic Republican Tradition*. Princeton: Princeton University Press, 1975. This is something of a classic. It provides a thorough medieval and Renaissance context for Machiavelli as a republican political thinker, then traces the influence of his thought in England and America. The book is quite difficult to read without a considerable amount of background.

Ridolfi, Roberto. *The Life of Niccolò Machiavelli*. Translated by Cecil Grayson. Chicago: University of Chicago Press, 1963. Despite many new entries, this biography is still considered "the classic."

Rubinstein, Nicolai. *The Government of Florence under the Medici, 1434–1494*. Oxford: Oxford University Press, 1966. This is a wonderful study of the political world into which Machiavelli was born and about which he wrote.

Skinner, Quentin. *Machiavelli: A Very Short Introduction*. Oxford: Oxford University Press, 1981 (reprint, 2000). Skinner's slim volume is a brilliant introduction to Machiavelli and his thought by a distinguished historian of political thought.

Strauss, Leo. *Thoughts on Machiavelli*. Chicago: University of Chicago Press, 1958. Strauss has little good to say about Machiavelli and the legacy he left the Western world.

Viroli, Maurizio. *Machiavelli*. Oxford: Oxford University Press, 1998. This is a thoughtful study of Machiavelli's ideas and not a biography. It is part of a distinguished series, *Founders of Modern Political and Social Thought*.

————. *Niccolò's Smile: A Biography of Machiavelli*. New York: Farrar Straus and Giroux, 2000. Here is Viroli's biography, well written and providing a positive assessment by a scholarly "fan" of Machiavelli.

Weinstein, Donald. *Savonarola and Florence: Prophecy and Patriotism in the Renaissance*. Princeton: Princeton University Press, 1970. This book is an interesting study of Savonarola, who fascinated Machiavelli and about whom Machiavelli comments in both *The Prince* and the *Discourses*.

Wilcox, Donald. *The Development of Florentine Humanist Historiography in the Fifteenth Century*. Cambridge: Harvard University Press, 1969. The title makes it clear that this is a useful book for understanding how Machiavelli's contemporaries understood and wrote about the past.

Internet Resources

"Discourses." *Constitution Society*. http://www.constitution.org/mac/disclivy.txt. Although not the most modern translation, this Web site reproduces the *Discourses* in English.

La Biblioteca di Babele. http://www.debibliotheca.com. Those who wish to test their Italian can look at several of Machiavelli's works in Italian by going to this Web site, clicking on Indice, then clicking on the letter M. Both the *Discourses* (*Discorsi Sopra la Prima Deca Di Tito Livio*) and *The Prince* (*Il Principe*) are here.

Letter from Niccolo Machiavelli to Francesco Vettori. http://econ161.berkeley.edu/Politics/Vettori.html. The famous letter from Machiavelli to Francesco Vettori describing his life in the country is found here.

"Livy." *Reed College.* http://academic.reed.edu/humanities/110Tech/ Livy.html#Texts. This is a useful site for learning about Livy and finding part of his *History of Rome* in English. The site also has a bibliography and links to other related Web sites. This is a good place to find useful background before reading Machiavelli's *Discourses.*

"Niccolò (di Bernardo) Machiavelli." *Brandeis University.* http://www.brandeis.edu/~teuber/machiavellibio.html. This Web site provides a basic biography and list of works.

"Nicolo [sic] Machiavelli (1459–1527): The Prince, 1513." *Medieval Sourcebook.* http://www.fordham.edu/halsall/basis/machiavelli-prince.html. This Web site contains *The Prince* and Machiavelli's life of Castruccio Castracani.

"The Prince." *Constitution Society.* http://www.constitution.org/mac/prince00.htm. Similar to the above Web site, this one provides an older translation of *The Prince.*

Notes

Notes